Photography by Ray Main

bridget bodoano

101 IDEAS

living rooms

quadrille

Editorial Director Jane O'Shea
Art Director Helen Lewis
Designer Paul Welti
Project Editor Hilary Mandleberg
Production Beverley Richardson
Photography Ray Main

First published in 2004 by
Quadrille Publishing Limited
Alhambra House
27–31 Charing Cross Road
London WC2H 0LS

British Library Cataloguing-in-Publication
Data. A catalogue record for this book is
available from the British Library.

ISBN 1 84400 090 7

Every effort has been made to ensure the
accuracy of the information in this book. In no
circumstances can the publisher or the author
accept any liability for any loss, injury or
damage of any kind resulting from any error
in or omission from the information contained
in this book.

Printed and bound in China

contents

part one
the big picture

part two
getting down to the detail

part three
keeping it fresh

part one

the big picture

what are you like? **five personalities in search of a living room**

What people require from their homes varies according to their needs, personalities and budget. You may dream of minimal heaven but this may not suit a young family; you may wish to fill your home with beautiful antiques, but your budget may not stretch that far. If you work from home, you may need somewhere that runs like an efficient and comfortable hotel, or perhaps a home that serves as an advertisement for you and your work. If you are always busy, your interior will probably be full of the paraphernalia associated with a life of activity. If you are the arty type your environment will contain objects and artefacts that are your treasures and inspiration. People who enjoy being surrounded by friends and family usually provide a welcoming ambience conducive to social gatherings, with the emphasis on comfort and accommodation. Those who love peace and quiet may benefit from a little Zen-inspired simplicity but can also find composure among a happy clutter of beloved possessions. When planning your living room make sure it suits you – not only in the look of the room but also in how it meets your lifestyle needs.

2

smart

You are fashion conscious and well informed, with an eye for new styles and directions. The ability to dress well follows through to a flair for putting together colours, textures and the right shapes to create a look that is smart and understated. You are confident using a basic, neutral palette of colours but know how to use flashes or splashes of colour and new accessories to bring a look bang up to date. Classic shapes, clean lines and good quality are all-important and simplicity is favoured above fastidiousness. Good taste prevails but you are capable of adding a 'Wow!' factor, whether in the form of bold use of colour, lighting, space and stunning materials or the subtle but clever addition of a single painting or a cashmere throw. Smart makes you feel good and impresses like-minded friends and, when necessary, work colleagues and contacts. You may be a fan of the new chic hotels, which combine pared-down stylishness with comfort, but you may also enjoy a little glamour. You probably prefer entertaining to socialising and the formality of a dinner party appeals more than the informality of dropping in. You know that looking good makes you feel good – and a smart, disciplined living room will have a similar effect.

smart aspirations

- clean lines
- minimalist tendencies
- design classics
- linen and flannel
- velvet and damask
- pale wood and limestone
- panelled walls
- steel and glass

casual 3

If you prefer jeans and trainers to suits and heels you may also prefer a more casual and relaxing environment in your living room. However, while wearing the wrong style of jeans or trainers has been known to damage your street cred, casual and relaxing in the home doesn't necessarily mean eschewing style, quality or fashion. Bring to your living room the sort of things you enjoy. You like the look and feel of soft and workmanlike fabrics and you appreciate well-made and practical objects – especially if, like a good pair of jeans, they get better with age. The result will be a room where you can feel at ease and create a relaxed, welcoming ambience.

casual influences

- denim
- cotton and linen
- fleece and knits
- comfort and warmth
- simple shapes
- easy living
- practical not precious

4 creative

As well as following the changing styles and fashions in interiors, arty people also enjoy keeping up with cultural trends. You are adept at putting together a personal style in both clothes and interiors that is unique, original and often influenced by the worlds of art and design. The look may contain historical references related to particular eras or styles through colour, pattern, paint effects and furnishings, and you are happy to include some examples of original works by you or your family. Combining different styles and elements can result in rooms that are busy and quirky yet charming, demonstrating an imaginative and lively mix of shapes and styles. You use a variety of sources for your individual look, perhaps mixing old and new, bargains and precious objects, chain-store buys with expensive designer pieces – a strategy that works well in interiors too. You will be adventurous with colour and materials and your living room is likely to be a place where you carry out creative pursuits surrounded by objects and possessions that demonstrate and stimulate your creative passions and instincts.

arty facts
- colour themes and collections
- pattern potential • antiques, modern and retro (sometimes blended)
- charleston farmhouse
- gallery chic • cultural influences

peace campaign
- natural colours and materials
- soft textures
- zen
- sound-proofing
- escape

peace lover 5

Even though you prefer the quiet life you may still be forced to live or work in the fast lane and therefore regard your home as a haven and refuge where you can relax and re-charge your batteries. If you live alone, a peaceful existence is more easily achieved, but even if you live in a busy, noisy household you will need to find somewhere, and some way, to create an oasis of calm away from the storm of activity. Perhaps you follow the tenets of Zen and enjoy applying them in creating harmonious interiors with natural materials and contents that are functional but also beautiful, in which case you are probably passionate about the environment and adopt an eco-friendly approach to your life, lifestyle and attitude to possessions. On the other hand, you may just be a private person who prefers your own company and curling up with a good book on a comfy chair in a charming, cosy boudoir surrounded by all of your favourite things.

activist 6

You seldom sit still and like to spend time on your various interests rather than relaxing. In your home, work surfaces and computer terminals, storage and shelving may be as important as sofas and soft furnishings, both for energetic enthusiasts and reluctant students. Hyperactivity is not always voluntary: it can be generated by the day-to-day comings and goings of family life, by the demanding frenzy of young children and the hectic, activity-filled timetables of school kids or the juggling of jobs and home life. If you are an enthusiastic participant in outside interests, your home may also become caught up in a whirl of activity for a diverse range of pursuits, from committee meetings and music making to posh parties and impromptu gatherings. Activists value flexibility, convenience, storage and well-organised space as a way of keeping their busy lives, and homes, under control.

active considerations
• efficiency • easy-care • hardwearing
materials • easy access • good facilities

who will use your living room? take a census

Making a note of who uses your living room, and when, will help you plan how to make the best use of the space and decide on a look that suits. If one of the following categories does not apply to you, devise your own!

single

More people than ever live alone. The advantage is that you only have yourself to please, but space in single-person dwellings is sometimes limited and therefore the living area may be small or may exist as an extension of the kitchen or bedroom. It may also have to double as working space and overnight accommodation for guests.

couple

In even the most harmonious relationships there can be conflict in matters of taste and the use of space. There may be the need for a little imagination and clever division of space in order to develop a scheme that accommodates the needs and preferences of both partners and offers the opportunity for doing things separately as well as together.

young family

Catering for a young family involves adopting a flexible approach. Providing a cheerful, safe environment for small children requires robust furniture and fittings, space to play and spread out, as well as cosy corners for quieter times. The needs of parents are equally important, but there are several ways to transform a lively daytime space into a restful evening refuge.

grown-up family

Older children still need space for their interests but they don't go to bed early, so families may find that a peaceful daytime room turns into a domestic version of a train station in rush hour later in the day. Peace has a greater chance if there is a designated space for work or hobby-related activities, provision for televisions, computers and sound systems, and plenty of comfortable seating.

sharer

Sharing accommodation with those who are not family or loved ones can be tricky, but a pleasant communal living area encourages household harmony and provides a place for socialising as well as serious discussion. Simple decor and a no-clutter policy will keep housework, and disputes, to a minimum.

how do you use your living room?

The high cost of housing means that space is at a premium and the luxury of a separate sitting room has become a thing of the past. Nowadays, during a typical week, the living room may be used as a place in which to eat, study, socialise, entertain, exercise, work, relax and even sleep. Each of these has its own requirements so if one room has to fulfil all these functions, it needs careful planning. Whatever you do, you must pinpoint how you want to use your living room. Do you require everyday comfort, evening sanctuary, weekend relaxation, special-occasion function room, entertainment headquarters, gymnasium, craft centre or romantic retreat?

If the living space is busy all day, every day, hardwearing, comfortable and robust furniture and furnishings will stand the pace. However, if you are out all day, the living room is often an after-hours place of refuge, in which case you can go for more luxurious materials. But although relaxation may be your room's primary function, you may also want it to include provision for a computer or hobby materials.

If your lifestyle means you are out most evenings, the living room may be empty except at weekends, when it becomes a special place to enjoy time relaxing, entertaining or doing something completely different. If this is the case, you may want to re-think your home and incorporate the under-used living room in another room.

relax

Having decided that your living room is first and foremost a place for you to relax after a day's work or to escape from hectic family life, use the following tips to make it a haven of tranquillity.

keep calm

Use a neutral palette and soft textures. For peace and well-being, try applying a little Zen-like harmony by using only natural colours and materials, and keep it simple as an uncluttered environment is less likely to distract you. Restrict the number of objects in a room and choose each item carefully, taking into account function as well as beauty and design. If it is not possible to devote a whole room to peaceful pursuits then find a corner of another one in which to seek solace.

keep the noise down

Use materials and furnishings that will absorb sound. Bare may be beautiful but it can be noisy so dampen the sound with carpet, rugs and soft furnishings and choose curtains or Roman blinds in thick fabrics. Book-lined walls can also help muffle the sound of noisy neighbours, but remember to be a good neighbour yourself and think twice before putting down bare floors in an upstairs flat, or placing your sound system too near a flimsy partition wall.

make yourself comfortable

Choose good-quality furniture that is generous in size and kind to your body. Before buying a sofa or chair test it out for comfort, allowing yourself space to stretch out. Don't overcrowd the room and make sure the temperature is comfortable. A chilly room will benefit from some heat and a real or flame-effect fire adds a cosy feel. To cool a room in warm weather, make sure the windows are in good repair and can be opened. For conservatories or large areas of glass, install blinds for shade and to prevent overheating.

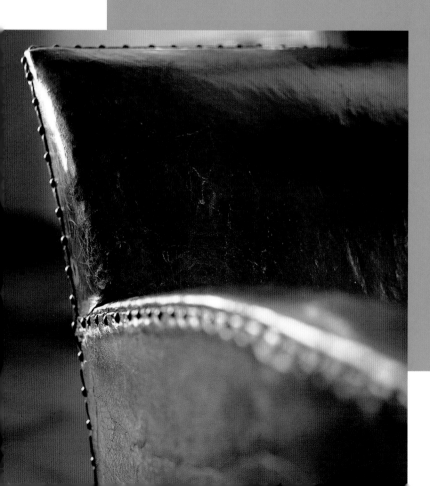

10

eat

Whether you want a living room that caters for family mealtimes or posh dinners, these ideas could get your tastebuds going.

family-sized

A generous table and comfortable dining chairs make for happy socialising eaters. A large table can also be used simultaneously for several different activities including homework, paperwork or even as a space for display.

shape up

Round tables are good for mealtime conversation and some fold in half and can stand against the wall to save room when not in use. Oval tables don't have sharp corners and take up less room than rectangular ones. Their curves also create a softer, more welcoming space.

individual portions

Happy snackers will appreciate the convenience of small tables, butler's trays and trolleys, and these are great surfaces for drinks and nibbles at parties too.

11

work

Work if you must, but don't allow work to dominate your life or your living room. These easy solutions for work, study and hobbies that have to be fitted into the living room could help save your and your family's sanity.

keep out

Avoid disasters such as damaged or lost work and equipment by defining the work area and, if necessary, keeping everything safely stowed away when not in use in lockable drawers and cupboards. In order to provide greater privacy for those who need to use the living area for work, homework or creative pursuits, divide the space by using permanent fixtures such as a shelf and low wall (see 30) or simple solutions such as a screen or curtain (see 31).

close to hand

Try to maintain discipline by keeping all work equipment and materials in one place, either on shelving or in drawers close by or in boxes on the table top. And always make sure that everything is put back in its proper place so there is no chance of it going 'walkabout' and cluttering up the rest of the living area.

main feature

An integrated hobby or work area need not be hidden away; in fact it could be turned into an interesting and attractive feature within the room. Shelves, noticeboards and samples of work all have decorative potential, as does the equipment itself (some PCs are much too smart to hide). Completed projects, the inspiration behind them and attractive storage solutions can all add interest and something unique to the decor of the living space.

socialise

You love to socialise and spend time entertaining your friends. These ideas will help to create a convivial atmosphere.

seating arrangements

Encourage relaxation and conversation by arranging sofas and chairs in friendly groupings and remember, perching on a dining chair is uncomfortable. Large floor cushions are fine for cosy chats or unexpected visitors.

table talk

The best dinner parties are sociable affairs where the conversation is as important as the food. If you entertain regularly, put your money towards a decent table and comfortable dining chairs so people are happy to sit.

kitchen confidential

Combined cooking, dining and living areas help ensure that all members of the household meet up at some point during the day. And if you do have a separate kitchen, it is nice to create a small, cosy space there with an armchair for unexpected guests, for anyone in need of a chat, or just a place for the cat.

exercise

Want to work up a sweat in your living room without messing up the furnishings? Exercise your brain with these tips.

space workout

Exercising requires room and unless you are a serious keep-fit fanatic with a dedicated fitness area, you'll need to clear a space. Keep furniture to a minimum and think wheels or castors.

fitness test

Exercise can seriously damage your decor, so be prepared to put down floor-protecting mats and check that floors and walls are strong enough to support equipment and the force that will be applied to it.

locker room

Large, heavy equipment, such as floor mats, exercise bikes and weights, needs stowing away when not in use. Weights can be kept in an attractive stout chest. Mats can be rolled up and kept in a tall cupboard, under the bed or in the corner of a cloakroom or bathroom. Keep larger items behind a sofa or screen, or just throw a beautiful rug over them.

romance 14

Create the right anbience and your living room can become the perfect place for injecting romance into your current relationship or for setting the scene for a new one if you wish.

comfort

It is difficult to be, or feel, romantic on uncomfortable furniture or in less than restful surroundings. A large comfy sofa, plenty of cushions and a deep pile rug offer a good base for a sensuous space, and even if you have minimalist tendencies you won't mind providing cashmere throws and the odd sheepskin. Be ready to turn up the heat, perhaps with an open fire, or make it possible to reduce the temperature if you must, with smart air-conditioning, an open window with billowing curtains, or a fan.

seclusion

Small rooms are conducive to intimacy and are perfect for privacy but it is not so easy to feel secluded in an open-plan setting no matter how glamorous the surroundings. If there are others in the house it will be even more important to find a romantic retreat for a little private passion. Closing off or containing a small area can be achieved in a variety of ways (see 19, 20, 30, 31), but whichever you choose, a little quietude will benefit your quality of life as well as your relationships.

close contact

Spontaneous romance is particularly appealing but is less likely to happen if the two of you are seated on separate chairs or at opposite ends of the room, so look at ways of arranging the furniture to encourage interaction and intimacy. Sofas and daybeds are more romance-friendly than chairs and even if you have a huge space, it is a lot cosier to place the seating in 'conversational' groupings. Making these areas as inviting as possible will encourage lounging and lingering and, who knows where that could lead?

15 private space or public arena?

While some of us thrive on hustle, bustle and plenty of people around, when it comes to their living room, others may prefer, or need, a little more peace, quiet and privacy.

public arena

If your living room is at the centre of a lively household, then ideally it should be big. If you don't have a large room, you can create one, either by using another room or part of the house as the living room (see 23) or by opening up an existing room (see 27). Open spaces mean living in a public arena, which has certain advantages: it looks and feels good, makes the most of the space available and encourages social interaction. Other advantages are being able to supervise young children while doing other things and plenty of space for entertaining. If you are a single occupant or have a less frenetic household, you may want to turn your room into a 'gallery space' for collections of paintings, furniture or ceramics or, alternatively, why not indulge in some minimalism and allow the space to speak for itself?

private space

Even the most gregarious people sometimes crave time and space to themselves. For those who spend their working day with others, a separate living room may be vital for re-charging their batteries. There are also other reasons for shutting yourself away, such as a need to concentrate on work, serious study or music practice. Equally, differing tastes in music, television programmes and friends often necessitate a private living space.

16

how to make a dual-use room work

Multi-purpose rooms will work better if you address the requirements of the space at the planning stage (see 29). Make provision for the location of sockets, aerials, lighting, storage and special equipment and investigate early on the practicalities of structural features such as changes in level or half-height walls, which you can use to divide the space (see 19). Many of these will need to be included in plans and instructions to builders. And to ensure everything will fit, check all measurements, not only of the space but also of furniture, fittings and equipment – as well as the length of your arms and legs.

prioritise

Decide which activity takes precedence. If a dining table is used infrequently then a fold-up version may be adequate. If the room doubles as your work space, plan the work area first and fit other activities around it.

mark out your territory

Clearly defined space makes it easier for more than one activity to take place at a time. Minimise disturbance and damage to work by putting up a physical barrier (see 30) or by keeping piles of papers, bulging boxes, sundry scraps and materials stowed away and out of sight in cupboards, drawers, chests or robust storage boxes. Locks will avoid tears and tantrums from children and grown-ups alike.

spatial harmony

A room where someone is trying to relax while another has to work is possible with imaginatively arranged furniture and space-dividing screens, shelving, curtains or even walls. Conflicts of interest can be solved by using headphones, placing humming computers and noisy equipment in a cupboard or on a rubber mat, or providing a supply of ear plugs!

keep it simple

A degree of unity will make a room look calmer as well as bigger.

• colour: keep things calm with a simple pale palette of not more than three colours. Use paint or fabric to unite a disparate collection of objects.

• furnishings: stick to one style or colour and match fittings to furnishings.

• materials: limit the range of materials; too many different elements will look too busy.

17 work to live

When your living room has to double up as the place where you earn your bread and butter, the following ideas will be the icing on the cake.

super efficient

Comfort and efficiency are key. Good lighting is a must as is room to sit at and use a computer, tools or machinery properly and safely. When planning, take into account ease of access, correct installation and positioning of equipment, plus storage of paperwork, materials and extras such as printers, scanners and fax machines (see 84).

separate lives

Your work area may look good (see 83) but the living room will be more inviting if work can be kept out of sight after working hours. Think about using a mix of shelving, partition walls, screens, cupboards, folding walls, blinds or curtains (see 22, 29, 30, 31).

privacy law

You may need to lay down rules to allow you privacy for phone calls, client meetings or just as an aid to concentration and inspiration. Grown-up housemates will (hopefully) respect your need to be alone but this can be more difficult with children.

18 part-time worker

Sometimes all you need is to be able to do some homework or indulge in a favourite hobby. These considerations will help you to combine occasional work with living-room life.

good connections

Home computers are a vital household tool for everything from simple e-mailing to serious study or paid work. Make sure there are adequate electric and phone sockets and that they are in the right place – if necessary, arrange for them to be professionally installed or moved. For neatness and safety, use plastic conduit to carry wires and cables under the floor or along the skirting board (see 84).

surface tension

If work is mainly paperwork or computer-based, your work surface won't be subjected to much wear and tear so you can go for glamour, but for activities involving glues, cutting tools and so on, you will need robustness. Laminates and linoleum can be scrubbed clean but wood, generously sealed and varnished, is also surprisingly tough. Use cutting mats and boards and protect the floor area.

sociable studies

Having a homework and hobby area in your living room encourages others to get involved – and this can create an atmosphere of nurture and mutual support that spills over into other areas of family life.

19

live to eat

If household arrangements mean you have to eat in the living room, make sure it is a pleasurable experience.

make room

A dining area works best when there is plenty of room for you to pull your dining chair out and get to your seat (see 82). If possible, keep the dining area separate from the sitting area and banish sofas and easy chairs to the other end of the room.

alternative treatments

Where there is not enough room for a conventional table and chairs, think restaurant/pub-style, with a fixed table and banquettes. You could screen them off with a half-height wall that also provides space for shelves, furniture or display (see 30), or consider a long, narrow table along one wall. This will take up even less room with benches either side rather than chairs.

space savers

Many chairs and tables fold up, out, down or away, and are perfect for casual dining or the occasional dinner party (see 82). Also look for small tables that open up, extend or lower to form larger dining or occasional tables.

20

day to night

There comes a moment in the life of every living room when it wants to go from hectic day to night-time relaxation.

light levels

Just turning off bright, general illumination and directional spots and downlights immediately creates a more soothing light level and lowers the tension. Work and clutter can disappear at the flick of a switch. Then you're ready for table lamps and gentle washes of light.

disappearing act

At the end of a busy day, conceal all evidence of work behind closed doors, a screen or curtain, and tidy away toys and other paraphernalia into baskets or boxes. You can also literally turn your back on daytime activities by positioning your sofa so it faces away from the work area.

creating an atmosphere

Reward yourself with some sensuality at the end of the day. Burn quality scented candles or essential oils, throw an apple log on the fire, open the windows to enjoy the scent of fresh air and evening flowers, soothe tired bodies with extra cushions or indulge in the luxury of a cashmere throw for tense shoulders.

21

guest accommodation

With careful planning, overnight accommodation need not inconvenience you, your guests or your living room.

bedding down

Providing a bed for the night for expected, and unexpected, guests is as simple as finding the right style of sofa bed, fold-up bed or inflatable mattress for your space, taste and budget (see 79). However, more imaginative and adventurous solutions include sleeping platforms and beds that fold away into the wall. Both will involve careful planning and the additional expense of getting professional advice for the feasibility, design and construction, but the final solution could save space and provide a talking point. A sleeping platform also provides unusual additional space for full-time occupants of the house.

a place for everything

Make visitors comfortable by providing storage for their clothes, belongings and bag or suitcase. Find somewhere to store bedding to keep the area free of unwanted clutter and thus make the room as useable as normal during the day and evening. Visitors will also feel that they are making less of an imposition on you and creating little disruption in your home. Look out for footstools that incorporate storage space, large chests and small storage units on wheels.

privacy provision

Open-plan layouts, glass doors and large un-curtained expanses of window make life difficult and a little too exposed for some overnight guests. Providing privacy can be a simple matter of adding a lock to the door so they can be spared unwanted intrusions, or pulling a blind or curtain across a glass door. However, if you live in a large, light and airy space you may have to provide other means of partitioning off the sleeping quarters. A folding screen is simple and a useful item to have anyway, but if you have frequent visitors you should consider making a more permanent arrangement for closing off an area, such as folding or sliding doors. These also play an important role in making a dual-use room work well.

one-room living

Living in one room means your space needs to be organised and clutter kept to a minimum otherwise areas that you want to keep separate will begin to overlap and confusion will reign. You might even consider employing an architect or interior decorator as they will be able to suggest unusual and unexpected ways of treating the space.

storage, storage, storage

Having a home for everything is a must. A wall of cupboards will present a calm face to the world yet house all the necessities of life. Store kitchen equipment and appliances at one end, clothing at the other, and work essentials in the middle.

good direction

Living in a single space leaves you no chance to escape to another room, so find ways to inject variety. Place seating to offer different views. Make the most of the light and view by placing a table, desk, armchair or sofa near the window. Have a seating area that faces away from the busy parts of the room and you will find it easier to relax. And remember that furniture doesn't have to be at right angles to the wall. Tables, work surfaces and seating on the diagonal can be more interesting and will free up unexpected areas for other uses.

different levels

A change in floor level breaks up the space by creating the suggestion of a collection of rooms and a raised area could be enclosed with walls or partitions. If the ceiling height allows, build a sleeping platform, or if it doesn't, raise the bed onto plan chests, cupboards or drawers to give extra storage space. Safety is key to the success of level changes so always get professional advice before planning anything structural.

good co-ordination

The space will look calmer if you keep to a strict scheme or theme with a restricted palette of colours and materials. Sticking to one style, whether antiques, fifties or strictly modern, will bring the whole scheme together, but if you are an inveterate collector and are bold and clever enough to create harmony out of chaos, you can break all the rules and come up with a look that's truly personal and completely different.

23

location and re-location

Open-plan living rooms are all the rage and dual-use living rooms are ideal for many situations. However, fashions and circumstances change, children grow up and living-room arrangements that used to work well can become intrusive or inconvenient. Have you the courage to re-define your living space? Start by taking a tour of your home and try to imagine it empty. You can allocate whatever activity you like to each room. Take into account any under-used or undeveloped spaces – including built-in cupboards, box rooms, conservatories, the roof space, landings and hallways. The aim is to ensure that every centimetre of space is being used to its full potential.

separate space

If taste or circumstances once led you to eschew the traditional 'front room', but if you are not short of space, then a separate living room may be just what you need now. It can be a haven of peace, you can furnish it in a style that is different from the rest of the house, and it offers a place where your 'best' treasures will be safe from the rigours of daily life.

upstairs or downstairs?

Living rooms are usually on the ground floor but they don't have to be. A basement area, especially one with access to a garden, would make a great living room. Or perhaps your bedroom has a sunny aspect and a pleasant view. Why not turn that into a living room – or even re-locate all your daytime activities to the top half of the house and use the ground floor for bedrooms?

nowhere/everywhere

With space at a premium, dedicating an area just to 'living' can be difficult, so why not create mini 'living pods' within other rooms – a sofa in the kitchen, a chaise longue in the bedroom, an armchair in the hall or bathroom?

an unusual 24
case for treatment

You have been through the exercise of imagining your home empty, just as it was when you first moved in (see 23), but you still can't quite see where that longed-for living room will fit. Now's the time to consider some more radical alternatives.

loft
Loft conversions are a great way of creating an extra room and maximising the unused, and often very large, roof space. Installing roof lights and/or dormer windows will transform it into a large, light and characterful space, which may make a fantastic living room. Make sure though that the rooms below won't be disturbed by noise from above.

garage
A solidly built garage can be lined and fitted out with new windows and doors for a relatively small sum and will make a perfect rumpus room or refuge. You could even link it to the rest of the house with a snazzy glass-enclosed walkway.

box room
Even a tiny, junk-filled box room can be converted into a cosy retreat for a spot of reclusive reading, television watching, music appreciation or just a little private contemplation.

hall
Maximise otherwise wasted space in a large hall by adding a sofa, comfy chair and a small table and desk. It could be all you need.

25
size matters

What makes a good-sized living room? You may think that a large space is best as it has room for all your furniture and possessions and you'll never, ever have to throw anything away. Or you may like the feel, of a cosy, intimate space. This is the moment to really assess the advantages and disadvantages of each.

the advantages of big

• it looks great

It is easy to be seduced by the fashionable and highly desirable 'light and airy look' and while it is more easily achieved in loft-style apartments or generous, beautifully proportioned rooms in properties of architectural merit, it is still possible to create the illusion of space in any living room. Even a small home can be transformed by judicious removal of walls.

• it feels great

Having more room can help reduce stress levels. Big spaces usually mean more windows and therefore more light, which is also important for well-being.

• it's sociable

A large, pleasant space is good for visitors and great for parties. It also encourages interaction: there is a better chance of a quick chat between busy people who are just passing through, and a large living room might even tempt the kids out of the confines of their well-equipped bedrooms. So unless you are a resolute recluse, choose big.

• it's comfortable

Sofas and armchairs take up a lot of space and it is difficult to relax if there is not enough room to stretch out. So if physical comfort's a top priority, you may want to go for big.

• it's best for action

Big rooms suit modern, busy lifestyles, with family and friends coming and going all the time and action packed into every minute of the day, while a small room may not be used because it's simply not up to the job. Two small rooms that are currently used for separate activities may work better and more efficiently if they are knocked into one big room (see 27).

the advantages of small

• it's a quiet retreat

At the end of a hard day it can be bliss to withdraw into the peace and quiet of a small haven away from the worries and clutter of other people and their activities. A small space can be made cosy and intimate with squashy, cosy furniture, or it can be a place for simplicity in your life when furnished with a bare, cell-like discipline. Either way, it could save your sanity.

• it's less expensive

As well as being cheaper to heat, a small space is also less expensive to furnish. You will need less furniture and the furniture can be on a smaller scale, which is more mainstream. Small also means it's less expensive to keep up with interior fashion and change your decor frequently if you choose.

• it's easier to decorate

Imposing a particular style or look on a small space is likely to be more successful than trying to unify disparate elements within a large space, so there is more incentive to experiment.

• it allows for indulgence

In a small room it is possible to indulge in a fondness for flowery wallpaper, expensive furniture, bright colours, loud music or eating chocolate without disturbing, offending or having to share your vices with other members of the family or household.

• it suits a crowd

Big spaces may look and feel wonderful but they do not suit all situations. Several smaller rooms may work better for crowded households.

• it means less mess

Spacious, immaculate homes in magazines often betray scant evidence of human life. There are no piles of washing-up and certainly no discarded trainers or half-eaten biscuits to sully the perfection. If you live alone or with people who are disciplined and fanatical about cleanliness, tidiness and design, then you may be able to keep a big space looking good, but for normal people and families, more space can mean more mess, so go for small.

• it's flexible

It is relatively easy to open up a space but more difficult to close it off again. The large space that is perfect now can, in a few years time, prove impractical and you will wish you had separate rooms. Remember, too, that opening rooms up can reduce the value of a property and make it more difficult to sell.

going for big 26

If you've decided that what you really really want is a big living room, you may have to make some structural changes, which means using the services of a professional builder and possibly a structural engineer or architect.

building regulations and planning laws

Even small works such as opening up a doorway may be subject to planning or building consent and of course, before embarking on extensions, conservatories, the conversion of roof spaces or garages, you should find out if you need planning permission. There may be strict regulations regarding space and its use, and privacy and light laws may affect the positioning of windows and new outside walls. Rules vary so ring you local planning department for guidance. If you live in a leasehold property, check to make sure that any work you plan is not in breach of your contract and if you live in a flat there may be a 'quiet enjoyment' clause which means that you cannot have bare floors, remove a wall or convert a roof space as it might result in increased noise that disturbs your neighbours.

major works

Any construction work is best left to a qualified builder who may also employ plasterers, carpenters, electricians and, if necessary, painters and decorators. If the work is extensive, it is worth employing an architect who will come up with ideas for design and materials that you may not have thought of. An architect can also take care of any planning application and oversee the entire project as well as supervise the builder.

If you wish to remove a structural wall you will need to consult a structural engineer, who will also make sure that any building regulation approval is obtained, and if you want to install a tiled, stone or concrete floor, it's best to ask the supplier to assess whether the existing floor structure is suitable for the added weight.

listed building or architectural gem

If your property is listed or of architectural merit you will require permission for any work and there may also be regulations regarding the use of correct or appropriate materials. Quality of workmanship may also be an issue and supervision and inspection of work may be imposed. An architect who has experience of listed properties or historic buildings will be able to offer design and specification advice and negotiate with the relevant official bodies or organisations. If your home is a good example of a certain architectural style or era, it should be shown some respect. There is no need to slavishly reproduce 'period details' or even retain them, but any interior will benefit from a sensitive approach to changes that might affect the original proportions and detailing of the building.

27

open up

Knocking down or through a wall can transform two ordinary rooms into one single stunning light-filled space. You may even want to open up an entire floor. But before you make such changes, be sure that your builder has checked the location of the supporting walls – you don't want to find the floor above is no longer supported.

dining

Modern informal living has largely made the dining room redundant so you could consider knocking down a wall to create a large living/dining space. If you are in two minds about the idea, compromise by connecting the rooms with double doors.

kitchen

Today's kitchen is often the favourite room in the home, so encourage people to gather there by opening it up to the living/dining space. This large, sociable room also suits informal entertaining. Cooking smells can be a problem but good ventilation should solve this.

hall

Removing the wall between a narrow hall and a pokey adjacent living room can give your home the open-plan look. Or you could create an unusual living area upstairs by combining a landing with a bedroom. Check though that this will not cause a noise or privacy problem with the other upstairs rooms, and make sure the front door is draught-proof.

conservatory

To make the most of light and outdoor views all year, why not remove the wall dividing the conservatory from the living area? Large expanses of glass can mean too much heat in summer and a chill in winter though, so invest in good-quality blinds that can be adjusted to ensure a comfortable ambience.

garden

Full-height folding glass doors instead of a wall between garden and living room give a dramatic, modern look. Large gas heaters on the patio and a glass canopy or awning will prolong your barbecue season well into autumn.

28 small is beautiful

Many of the suggestions in One-Room Living (see 22) apply to small rooms but where small really means small, the following ideas are sure to give your small living room some really big ideas.

keep it small

A small room will look more spacious if you keep the furniture and furnishings small too. Don't buy anything until you have checked the measurements in relation to your room: furniture that looks quite small in a large store can look huge once it is in your home. As homes become smaller, more manufacturers are offering ranges of small-scale furniture that are both well designed and comfortable.

keep it simple

Unless you want to go outrageous (see Be Outrageous, below) a simple decorative scheme works best for a small room. Stick to a palette of pale or neutral tones, with perhaps just one wall in a bold colour, and restrict the use of pattern to one wall of wallpaper, one item of furniture or just the curtains and blinds. If you want to use a number of patterned wallpapers and fabrics, then make sure they are all within a similar colour range and don't use too many big prints.

harmony

A small room will benefit from the principles of Zen where balance and harmony are created by an un-cluttered environment and the use of natural colours and materials. Think bare windows and floors, unbleached cottons and linens and a single flower. Limit the number of objects in the room, keeping only those that look beautiful and work well. A little feng shui can help you arrange them to best advantage.

keep it clear

If you love minimalism you will already be well versed in the principles of Zen and feng shui and will revel in the purity of virtually empty space, but even if you prefer a busier environment your small room will benefit from a few breathing spaces. Keep the walls clear to make the room feel bigger and also try to keep all surfaces, especially floors, as unobstructed as possible and make sure they stay that way with regular de-cluttering sessions.

keep control

A place for everything and everything in its place may be an ideal that normal life makes difficult to achieve but if you provide somewhere to put things, it may encourage you, and other household members, to keep the place tidy. Good storage for newspapers, magazines, CDs, DVDs and so on are a good start.

wall space

Storage can be a big problem in a small space. Look for unusual alternatives, such as hanging your furniture or possessions Shaker-style on a row of pegs or using wall-mounted, fold-down seating, tables and work-surfaces. Hide clutter in nearly invisible, ceiling-height, shallow cupboards with plain doors painted the same colour as the walls.

10 ideas

optical illusion

Mirrors not only make a room seem bigger they also reflect the light, but position them carefully – it is disconcerting to find you are constantly looking at yourself or seeing double. If possible keep mirrors behind you, or at an angle, and place them high to avoid too much eye contact. A large window area and glazed or partly glazed doors and walls allow in more light and open up a space psychologically if not physically.

concentrate and consolidate

If you love to surround yourself with treasured collections and other bits and pieces, keep them in orderly groups rather than random scatterings. A wall of shelves filled with books and various objects can also accommodate the television, computer, videos, CDs and much more, freeing up the other walls for pictures or displays or just to be relaxing blank spaces.

indulge

A small room is the perfect place for you to indulge in a little luxury that would be too expensive or impractical elsewhere. Buy one enormous, expensive or extravagant modern chair or sofa and fulfil your aspirations with a solid wood-block floor, a beautiful handmade rug or deep-pile carpet in 100% wool. Cover the windows with made-to-measure shutters and blinds or curtains in a beautiful or glamorous fabric. Furnishing a whole house with your favourite antique, designer or retro look may cost too much and be overwhelming, but used in a small room it can be surprisingly inspirational.

be outrageous

Small rooms are perfect for experimenting with deep colours, dynamic patterns, wild styles or mad ideas – and if it all proves too much and makes your head spin, it is less expensive and less trouble to put right.

draw up a plan

Before finally deciding on what you want to do with your living area it is sensible to draw a plan of the room, or rooms, involved. Measure carefully and using squared paper (or a computer programme) draw a floor plan which includes all walls, positions of doorways, windows, heaters, radiators, fireplaces, light sources and fittings, electric sockets, telephone terminals and anything else which might affect layouts, arrangement of furniture and the overall design. Work out which way the windows face so that you know where the sun comes in, and mark in the compass point.

Make templates of the individual items of furniture and fittings you are planning to use, including anything that you are thinking of buying. Shops, suppliers and catalogues usually provide dimensions but if not ask them to take measurements, or do it yourself. Include templates of shelves or work surfaces that are to be included in the scheme even if they are to be fixed to the wall.

Draw additional templates that include the space needed for using the item of furniture – sometimes things that appear to work well on paper don't work in practice. For dining furniture, desks and worktops include the space required for chairs, remembering that you need extra space for pulling them out and actually sitting down. Calculate the leg room required for stretching out and add it to the dimensions of the sofas and armchairs. For cupboards and other storage furniture add space for opening or pulling out doors, drawers or sliding shelves.

Playing around with the templates, and trying the plan with different colours and fabric swatches, will help you to refine your thoughts on how to arrange things. It will also alert you to any structural or service requirements such as building works, wiring, heating and so on, and will enable you to organise them well in advance.

the physical divide

A single space can be divided up in a variety of ways from solid walls to invisible divides.

walls

Choose from a stud partition wall that is easy to install or a brick or blockwork wall, depending on style and structural requirements. Other options include clear or etched glass and glass bricks, either alone or as part of a solid partition. Another alternative is a 'floating' wall, offering privacy without impeding the light. It could end just short of the ceiling or at worktop level, in which case you can use the top of the wall as a shelf.

doors and panels

Ideal for spaces that you only want to close off at certain times, full-height doors open the space up most. Folding doors allow the whole wall to be folded away, while sliding wall panels are great for a quick change of scene.

furniture and screens

Shelves, bookcases, cupboards, chests – even a long bench or table – can be used to divide a space. Open shelves can be accessed from both sides and don't obstruct the light. Screens, from the simplest office-style variety to designer models, offer another easy, flexible and often inexpensive solution.

blinds and curtains

Slatted, roller, and Roman blinds hung from the ceiling are a simple way to screen off an area. Curtains soften the look of the space and hide away any mess. They are also good for keeping draughts out and warmth in.

floor levels

A change of floor level – from raised areas and high sleeping platforms to sunken seating – makes a dramatic space divider, but be mindful of safety (see 22).

the virtual divide

Walls and partitions are not the only way to delineate the use of space; separation can be created with just a change of mood.

furniture and style

Arrange the furniture into mini-'rooms' so there are clearly defined areas for separate activities, or use different styles – hard-edged functionality for a workspace, a softer look for the relaxation area.

colour and light

Colour-code your activities, using subtle changes of tone or bold contrasts. Similarly, use bright, general lighting for work areas and low light for relaxation. A lighting track or group of downlights highlights the division of space.

floor finishes

Map out the space using carpet for a seating area but a hardwearing, bare floor finish for work areas. Rugs make good 'islands' on which to create separate rooms.

32 colour scheming

Deciding on a colour scheme can be confusing as there is so much choice. Whether you are building on what you already have or starting from scratch, it will help if you gather together a collection of swatches, materials and inspiration to help put together your personal palette. Although you can get ideas by looking through books and magazines on interiors, broaden your horizons and find inspiration in art and fashion – perhaps you have a favourite designer or painter. A visit to a gallery can spark a revelation – buy lots of postcards chosen for colour as well as style of painting. Collect as many colour charts and samples of fabrics, wall coverings, floor finishes and materials as possible and put them all together in a big shallow basket, bowl or box. Throw in extras such as the postcards, pictures cut out of magazines, pebbles, bits of driftwood and anything else with personal colour appeal such as balls of wool or sewing thread, a woolly hat, a favourite pot or even fruit and veg. Don't confine yourself too soon to one colour direction: put together a number of collections with different colour themes and see which emerges as the favourite. Using a variety of objects not only highlights the range and subtlety of colours and textures but also makes it easier to identify the colours and materials that don't blend well.

33 radical change or modest modification?

Whether you decide on a completely fresh start for your living space or a modification of what you have will depend on budget, time, your current furniture and furnishings, and how much energy and patience you have. It may be well worth disrupting the household in order to gain your ideal living space and bold decisions, imagination, extensive or minor building works and a well-thought-out decorative scheme can change your life as well as your home. However, if you can't, or just don't want to embark upon anything too major, don't forget that by using only a single tin of paint and re-arranging the furniture, a room can be totally transformed.

practical pointers for decorating success

be prepared
It is time-consuming and tedious, but good preparation is the key to a good finish. Have any plastering, electrical or plumbing work done before starting any decoration.

safety first
Read all instructions carefully and wear gloves, masks and goggles. Take care lifting heavy weights, handling materials, working on slippery floors and using tools.

stripping out
If you are starting from scratch, enjoy stripping the room back to basics by removing old wall and floor-coverings, unwanted fixtures and fittings, damaged woodwork and loose plaster.

get stripping
Strip old wallpaper using warm water, wallpaper stripper or a steamer, and old paint using a blowlamp or paint stripper. All loose flakes of paint must be scraped off and rubbed down.

get filling
Fill holes in walls and woodwork with a proprietary wall and/or wood filler.

rub down
For woodwork it is important to provide a 'key' for the paint to adhere to. Prepare surfaces using a combination of power tools or a selection of abrasive papers, pan scourers, wire wool and brushes.

wash down
Wash all walls. Use warm water with a squeeze of mild detergent or, for stubborn dirt and grease, a stronger proprietary product. Don't forget to clean behind pipes and in awkward corners.

sealing
Seal any damp patches with stain sealer (but try to cure the problem first). Apply wood or metal primer to bare wood and metal, and treat dusty or flaky surfaces with stabilising primer. Prime any new plaster.

quantity survey
Work out what you need and buy enough as different batches of paint, wallpaper and fabrics can vary slightly.

protection
Protect floors and furnishings with dustsheets, newspaper, polythene or a combination. Spills will soak through dustsheets and newspaper, so put polythene underneath for extra protection.

2
part two

getting down to the detail

35
choosing colour

Colour affects not only how a room looks and feels but how you feel too. It can make a room look big, small, peaceful or lively and can cheer us up, calm us down or energise our flagging spirits. Unless you live alone there will be other people's tastes and preferences to be taken into consideration so it is important that the colour choice suits all. Choosing colour for dual-use living spaces needs careful thought, too. If you use a room for work or hobbies and need a high level of illumination, a dark, dramatic colour will absorb too much light may and may be be too oppressive for long periods of time. A multi-function room will look bigger and calmer if the same colour is used throughout but using a subtle or contrasting colour for the living area will help define the space and enable you to switch off from the activities associated with work areas. Practical and personal requirements may preclude bold experiments but a dash of colour lifts the mood and can be incorporated in many ways from one wall to a single cushion or vase.

colour do's and don'ts

do choose colours you like as your emotional response is important and reflects your personality.

don't choose a colour just because it's fashionable.

do take into account the style and proportions of the room and the colour of the materials and fabrics in it.

don't be afraid to experiment with paint colour. Paint is relatively inexpensive so mistakes can easily be covered up.

do consider the light: what looks great on a sunny day can look grim on a grey one, and a subtle hue in daylight can turn into an unpleasant sludge in artificial light. You should always test paint colours on more than one wall.

don't use colours that draw attention to defects and unattractive features like ugly windows and pipes.

do look at the colour in context, not just against white. Cut the paint chips from the chart and try them against the other colours in your palette.

do take your time and don't rush into any decisions.

don't let colour distract from beautiful architecture, furniture, objects or views and don't create a situation where colours fight for attention. If you have colourful furnishings and possessions, keep the background plain. If your possessions are not quite up to scratch, blend them into a background that complements or reflects their colouring.

colour charts

Paint suppliers and manufacturers now produce colour charts and brochures that present colours in an informed and helpful way, putting them into stories and categories based upon mood, tone, historical or design context. As the colours within a single category share similar characteristics, a group chosen from the same family will naturally work well together.

heritage and history

Whether your home is a genuine historical gem or you just admire styles from the past, historic paint ranges will help you add a touch of authenticity. Based on careful research not only into the colours but also the pigments and materials used at the time, these colours and paints enhance the inherent properties of an old building and bring subtlety to new ones.

whites, neutrals and naturals

White is no longer just white, it now comes in huge range of variations from the dirty greenish tinges of old limewash to the pristine blue-tinted freshness of brilliant white. Neutrals, far from being indifferent or dull, bring sophistication as well as peace and harmony. Their palette includes off-whites, beiges, greys, soft pale greens and blues, many of them colours associated with un-bleached fibres and materials such as stone and wood, but other colours from nature also, the darker hues of slate, forest green and sea blue and the deep natural pigments of vegetable dyes.

design and fashion collections

A number of designers and organisations collaborate nowadays with paint and fabric manufacturers to bring out their own colour collections, which feature the latest must-have colours as influenced by the worlds of fashion, art and interiors. These collections are great and save hours of agonising over whether you have chosen the exact shade as seen on the catwalk, in that up-market magazine or as used by the latest hot artist.

37 pattern pending

The fashion for a simple, smooth, pared-down look has made people apprehensive about using pattern but it is perfect for adding variety and personality to a room. Pattern is often introduced in fabrics and wallpaper but other sources include rugs, carpets, decorated furniture, stencils, wall hangings, pictures and ceramics. Subtle prints in soft or muted colours are easy to incorporate but large patterns and bright colours will have a bigger impact.

mixing and matching

Patterns work well together if they share the same colour palette. Co-ordinated ranges with plains and prints in paint, wallpaper, fabric and tiles are fine if you limit your choice to two or three elements, but can be unsubtle if you opt for more. On the other hand, certain collections are very restrained and need an injection of something bolder to lift them, perhaps a contrasting colour or print. If you have gathered together samples of colours, materials and objects (see 32), use them as the inspiration for new combinations – they will look more spontaneous than if you rely on off-the-peg options.

One way of ensuring colour harmony with a mixture of plains and patterns is to use a monochromatic colour scheme: tones and shades of one colour or a single colour plus white or ecru look sophisticated. If your pattern is to appear in the fabrics, then a collection of blue and white, red and white or black and white that mixes traditional florals, spriggy prints and toiles de Jouy as well as checks, spots and stripes works particularly well, especially with plain white or unbleached cottons and linens. If you are using wallpaper, stick to just one pattern, perhaps as a feature wall (see 68) and make sure other patterns harmonise, either through their style or colour. If you have a patterned carpet, be prepared to use similar colours and tones in the rest of the furnishings, and unless you are confident or feeling reckless, keep them mostly plain.

The designs of a specific era – a collection of fifties or sixties prints, a muted selection of Art Deco geometrics or a nostalgic assemblage of pretty flower prints and chintzes – share a common style. Similarly the simple patterns and natural vegetable dyes of ethnic fabrics and fibres mean they blend well together and the intrinsic character of oriental carpets makes it possible to use several in one room despite their variation in designs and colourings.

Brighten and lift a neutral colour scheme with flashes or dashes of colour and pattern. Very big, bold or bright are best. Confine them to one area or feature such as curtains, one wall, a rug or a single armchair.

38 texture

Combinations of smooth and textured finishes add variety, definition and contrast to a living room. Including textured weaves in a group of fabrics of similar colour will produce subtle tone changes that also gives a colour scheme more life. Even a minimal monochromatic interior can be full of contrast with a range of finishes from the shiny smooth surfaces of glossy paint to the rougher appearance of exposed brick or raw wood. Exploring and exploiting the textural differences in similar materials, such as plain and etched glass or shiny and brushed stainless steel, will add sophistication, while rougher contrasts emphasise character and give definition to spaces and colours. The fashionable bare and industrial looks make the most of coarser, uneven textures while those used for smarter looks are subtler and more uniform. Different materials have varying textural characteristics and modern interiors use them in an ever-changing and unexpected variety of ways. The industrial look has obvious contenders but the smoothest looks also include a few coarse textures.

textures for industrial chic

- exposed brick
- rough wood
- bare plaster
- distressed paint surfaces
- slate
- wrought iron
- galvanised metal
- concrete floors

textures for sleekly smart

- brushed stainless steel
- glass
- matt plastic
- furry fabrics
- hairy tweed and knits
- embossed rubber and metal floors
- gloss paint
- limestone

39

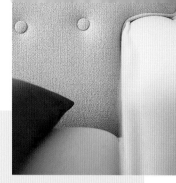

choosing a style

suits you?

If you have done the personality checks in Part 1 (see 2 to 6) you will already be prepared to let your own personality influence your chosen look and give you the confidence to put together your own inimitable style. If, however, you are a trend junkie and need to toe the latest line in fashion, then by all means follow the in-crowd.

suits your home?

If you have a beautiful, period home you will want to decorate in a style that is sympathetic, but don't get hung up on authenticity, which may not suit your lifestyle and tastes. Even if your living room isn't an architectural masterpiece bear in mind the proportions and be prepared to celebrate good features and play down less attractive attributes.

is it practical?

You may well aspire to the open-plan, all white, minimalist look but if you live a normal life and share your living space with others less aspirational than you it could be that pristine perfection soon turns into a finger-marked mess: bare floors and windows look fabulous but only if

they are draught-proof; natural floor coverings look great but stain easily; open shelves gather dust. Anticipate the pitfalls as well as the positives and adjust accordingly.

is it achievable?

While it is important to do things properly and not be afraid to be adventurous, make sure your plans are not too ambitious. For large-scale projects involving new floors and building works make sure that your builder or craftsman is up to the job. Take professional advice to ensure that what you are planning is legal, structurally sound and do-able (see 26).

is it affordable?

Decorating, especially if building or installation work is involved can turn out to be much more expensive than anticipated. Even the best-laid plans have a habit of exceeding the original budget so make sure that you have budgeted for every stage of the job: 'little' extras can soon add up to large sums. The cost of basic materials may be low but getting a builder or other professional to turn them into walls, floors and finished projects is a costly business (see 26).

5 ideas

new modern 40

The term 'Modern' is generally applied to furniture and design that is free of unnecessary ornament and has a pared-down quality with emphasis on spaces and simple shapes. Several modern design classics date back to the first half of the 20th century with designers such as Charles Eames and Arne Jacobsen still extremely popular and fashionable today. This was also the era of architect Mies van der Rohe's concept of 'Less is more', which is very relevant right now with the new modernism represented in plain walls, an un-cluttered environment and an atmosphere of calm order (the perfect antidote to the hectic whirl of full and busy lives). The 'loft' look epitomises the essence of new modern interior design with space and light as the most important ingredients. The commercial buildings recently converted into apartments have also introduced industrial materials and finishes such as exposed brick, concrete and galvanised steel. Achieving this look in more modest sized rooms and homes involves cutting down on the contents and keeping things light with pale coloured walls, bare floors and minimal window coverings. White or neutral tones, light-coloured wood and liberal use of glass will also help.

If this disciplined approach is a little too impersonal and clinical for your taste then take a look at the newest trends inspired by the seventies and influenced by Scandinavian design. The feel is warmer with richer colours and wood finishes and injections of bold colour and pattern. Look for wood-panelled walls, curvaceous shapes in plastics and bent plywood, furry rugs and even shag-pile carpet.

new modern elements

- curved plywood
- wood panelled walls
- long, low sideboards
- shag-pile rugs
- coloured tweed
- beige and brown
- orange and leaf green
- Scandinavian design classics

icons

- Charles Eames recliner and footstool designed in 1956
- Arne Jacobsen 3107 'Butterfly' chair designed in 1955
- Barcelona Chair designed by Mies van der Rohe in 1929
- Tulip Chair by Eero Saarinen designed in 1955–6
- Pendant lights by Paul Henningsen designed in the 1950s

affordable chic

It is now possible to find a huge range of affordable furniture and accessories that are extremely well designed, making it possible for anyone on a limited budget to create a modish look for their home. Low-price furniture is mass-produced, sold through large chains and therefore widely available, so in order to prevent a homogenous or instantly recognisable style it is wise to take a few precautions. Stick to plain, simple designs and avoid 'imitations' as they seldom live up to the original. Keep away from fancy details, which can look unconvincing and tacky, and choose plain fabrics in whites and neutrals – other colours usually lack subtlety and intensity and easily identified prints announce clearly where they were bought. Cheap can look chic and expensive if you use imagination and borrow a few tricks from smart fashionistas who mix designer labels with high-street bargains to give their best-buys a touch of extravagance or glamour. As with clothes, it is fun to create your own variation on a style and while the best affordable furniture and furnishings are those that fall into the plain and simple category, there is no reason why you shouldn't be able to create the latest fashionable look or dress them up as something more sophisticated or quirky.

The fashionable industrial look provides plenty of opportunity for cheap chic as many of the raw materials are inexpensive and can be sourced directly from DIY stores, builder's merchants and commercial suppliers. Be alternative and use office furniture and fittings, catering equipment, photographers' lights and industrial shelving. Use galvanised steel finishes, unfinished wood, sheets of plywood and chipboard, and industrial floor finishes such as cord carpeting and concrete.

five cheap tricks

1 • Dress up inexpensive sofas and chairs with stylish accessories such as wool and cashmere throws, silk cushions, sheepskin or leather cushions.

2 • Tone down new, too-bright wood by wiping over with finishing oil mixed with a very small amount of darker wood stain and use a similar technique for achieving a uniform wood colour on a range of different pieces.

3 • Unify a disparate collection of furniture by painting each piece in a single colour or range of similar tones and smarten up a disorderly collection of upholstered furniture with new covers in similar, or co-ordinating, fabrics and colours.

4 • For an expensive, antique look, paint whitewood or MDF furniture in specialist colours then apply crackle glaze (available at craft shops and DIY stores).

5 • Less is more: don't get carried away with the cheapness, buy two slightly more expensive things rather than several very cheap ones. And don't overcrowd a room: cramped conditions will emphasise any shortcomings in quality and design.

grown-up luxury

There comes a time, perhaps the children have left home or you find yourself in comfortable financial circumstances, when you have the resources and the inclination to do things properly and invest in home improvements that put quality and a touch of luxury at the top of the list. This is the time to indulge in the furniture, furnishings and interior style that you have hankered after for years. Grown-up luxury allows you to eschew fickle and fast-changing fashion – this is a style that is defined by quality and attention to detail rather than any specific design or colour theme.

Take the opportunity to look at all aspects of your living room interior, including the condition of the basic structure. Decide whether you want to spend time and money making it perfect with building works such as opening up walls, re-plastering or re-wiring, and perhaps putting in new windows or laying a new floor. Think about installing a sophisticated lighting or sound system, or a new fireplace. Take out old cupboards and shelves and replace them with craftsman-made, bespoke shelving and storage. Instead of making do with off-the-peg fittings, go for made-to-measure blinds and curtains with quality fittings and track systems. Investigate luxury wall coverings, not only authentic paints but hand-printed paper, wood panelling and even silk. Choose luxury materials such as

limestone, slate, solid oak and leather. Choose your favourite furnishing styles and include a seriously comfortable chaise longue along with the sofas, armchairs, footstools and occasional tables. Pay a little extra for high quality, beautiful fabrics: heavy linens, velvets, smooth wools and silk damasks. If you have a living/dining space why not consider a new, elegant dining table and chairs and perhaps a sideboard filled with beautiful table linen and glasses? Classical shapes, good antiques and modern design classics will never date – but buy the genuine article rather than an imitation, and marvel at its qualities. Get down to the details and replace prosaic lamps and light fittings with beautiful alternatives – and change the light switches too. Invest in an oriental rug or a new, hand-tufted modern design.

grown-up luxuries

- daybeds and chaise longues
- leather club chairs
- glass-fronted bookcases
- drinks cupboards
- bespoke storage
- made-to-measure curtains, blinds and covers
- integrated lighting and sound systems
- antiques
- wood block floors

43 retro

Retro is all the rage and some people go to great lengths to recreate the styles of the past with original furniture and accessories plus all the authentic colours and materials. Art Deco has distinctive geometric shapes but subtle colours, the fifties can be quite wild and the sixties bring back bright primary colours and geometric flowers. Colours were a little more sombre in the seventies – an era that included a wide range of styles from pine kitchens to Punk, but also had a sub-plot of some of the best Scandinavian design.

If you are a retro buff then you know what to go for and how to put it together, but don't get carried away by 'authenticity', which can look too contrived. Instead, use references: the colours, materials and shapes that reflect the character of the era. Even if you have only one good example, such as a fabulous fifties table, put it against a chewing-gum pink wall and you have your fifties look.

art deco
- warm soft greens, beiges, cream and light blue
- squares and circles
- rounded corners
- matt finished oak or distinctive polished grains such as walnut
- chrome and tubular metal
- mirrored surfaces

fifties
- sugared colours
- melamine and plastics
- rounded feet on furniture and fruit bowls
- abstract designs based on science and nature
- Cadillac style
- studio couches

sixties
- primary colours
- geometric flower prints
- plain, simple shapes
- brightly coloured plastics
- open shelves
- floor cushions

seventies
- French country kitchen style
- basketware
- cork
- shag-pile carpet
- Scandinavian design
- long, low sideboards

44

comfy casual

The fact that you believe a home is for living in doesn't mean you don't care how it looks, but you also want comfort, practicality and convenience. Casual style options include the re-invented country cottage, stripped of unnecessary frills and fabric. It has bare floors, large pieces of furniture and big armchairs and it is the perfect place for shabby chic – faded chintz, distressed finishes and rough surfaces. No need to worry about uneven plaster or less than perfect paintwork. Just wash them down and apply a coat of paint. Scrub old stone or wooden floors and leave them as they are.

'Nostalgic eclectic', with its homely utilitarian furniture of the thirties and forties, is another casual style. Evidence of wear and tear adds to the charm and slightly battered painted furniture is de rigueur. This fashion heralds a refreshing, relaxed and personal approach to home style, so take a new look at your belongings and instead of throwing them out enjoy them for their familiarity. It may be that your new-look living room is lurking beneath the old one and only requires some serious de-cluttering, a wash and brush up and perhaps a fresh coat of paint.

Closet couch potatoes will opt for a superb home-entertainment system, huge squashy sofas and deep armchairs, lots of cushions, a relaxing ambience, plus a good supply of books, magazines and newspapers.

contemporary cottage

- antique linens
- faded chintz
- painted country furniture
- bare wooden or stone floors

nostalgic eclectic

- old school furniture
- painted cupboards
- Formica or enamel top tables
- utility furniture

couch potato

- extra large sofas
- cushions and throws in woolly knits and fleecy fabrics
- floor cushions
- high-quality home-entertainment equipment

45 indulgent

Not everyone enjoys living a pared-down, uncluttered life so if you hanker for more rather than less, why not indulge in a little sensuality, romantic exoticism and excess? This can be anything, from a little bit hippy to unashamedly boudoir, but whatever you go for it will probably be feminine and definitely not minimal. There are plenty of markets, boutiques and second-hand shops to browse in for goods and inspiration; foreign travel increases the selection and the chance of a bargain. Look for Eastern and ethnic influences including embroidered fabrics, wall hangings, small items of furniture and pots. Hunt through antique markets for lace curtains, fringed silk shawls and old fabrics, especially florals and velvets. Enjoy a little 'maximalism' but take care not to overdo it or you will end up with a living room that looks fussy; if you don't want to go all the way, give your treasures some breathing space and allow them to stand out against simple, plain backgrounds and team them with clean-lined, modern furniture and lighting. Arty types will enjoy mixing colours and patterns and may be tempted to paint their own decorations on furniture and walls. If all this excess is too much for you why not break yourself in gently and for now just drape a beautiful embroidered, fringed silk shawl over the back of the sofa.

exotic/hippy

- daybeds, cushions, drapes
- rich, brilliant, jewel-coloured silks of the East
- indigo and shocking pink Indian fabrics
- sari fabrics, embroidery, mirrors
- hot, earthy Moroccan colours spiked with blue
- chinese prints in bright reds and greens often used with black
- oriental rugs and kelims

boudoir/salon

- velvet-covered sofas, curvy chairs and chaise longues
- purples, dark red, deep blue and greens
- creams, dusky pinks, watery blues and eau-de-nil
- heavy lace and beaded curtains
- tablecloths, fringed shawls and lampshades
- chandeliers and pretty glass lamps
- screens
- chinoiserie

romantic/feminine

- pretty prints, cabbage roses and chintz (it's back) and toile de Jouy
- soft linens and crisp cottons, seersucker and voile
- soft pastel pinks, blues and lavender; strawberry pink and bright turquoise
- pretty shaped chairs and perhaps a few frills

arty

- old battered furniture
- distressed paint surfaces
- patchwork and appliqué
- wall hangings
- hand-painted decoration on walls and furniture
- artworks
- collections of found objects

46 temperature control

No matter how beautiful your surroundings, you will not be able to relax in a living room that is too hot or too cold. It is important to get the heating right, and how you do it will depend on what is practical and cost-effective for your home as well as what impact it makes on the interior. Central heating is now an accepted comfort of modern life and a good system will maintain a constant temperature throughout the year. Underfloor heating and warm-air systems are virtually invisible but radiators and panel heaters aren't so they should be chosen and positioned carefully. Choice of fuel depends on availablity as well as cost and convenience, but whatever type of heating you opt for, make sure you employ experts to install it. And don't forget, many living rooms are once more featuring a good, old-fashioned open fire for looks and cosiness.

pipework, boilers and wiring

Central-heating systems comprise combinations of boilers, pipework, cables, time clocks, thermostats and control panels, which should ideally be kept out of sight. Pipes and cables are normally concealed under the floor and anything above ground level enclosed in plasterwork, wall spaces, boxed-in panels or conduit. Boilers are often sited in the kitchen or utility room, but sometimes in the bathroom or in a cupboard, but try to site them away from the action as the noise from burners, pumps, fans and thermostats can be intrusive. Gas boilers need to be vented and must therefore be placed on an outside wall. Always employ a registered installer for these.

ventilation

It makes economic sense to ensure that expensively produced heat is not allowed to escape through badly fitting windows and doors, but it can be unhealthy – and even dangerous – to seal yourself in. 'Adequate' ventilation requires that the air in our homes changes at least ten times a day to avoid the build-up of pollutants such as fungi, viruses and VOCs (volatile organic compounds). That's as good a reason as any to open a window! There are strict regulations concerning ventilation, which is why it is essential to check with a professional that your home complies. Poor ventilation has a serious effect on our health, producing headaches, making us feel sleepy and generally unwell, and creating an unhealthy environment for asthmatics. Lack of air increases humidity and is often the cause of condensation and mildew, but excess heat creates a dry atmosphere, which dries out wood and makes it warp. Close proximity to a heat source can ruin furnishings, and may also be a fire hazard, so make sure furnishings don't come into contact with radiators, panel heaters, warm air vents or fires.

three winter warmers

1 • draught excluders

Draughts have a habit of sneaking in and taking the edge off cosy. Keep them out with long, heavy, lined curtains pulled across windows and doorways. High-backed sofas and wing chairs will also help to keep you warm.

2 • all in the mind

Colour can be used to send out subliminal messages that warm us up psychologically. Our emotional response to colour makes it possible to counteract a chilly atmosphere with warm tones which will, in turn, make us feel comfortable and relaxed and therefore warmer (see 35).

3 • dress up

Some say it is healthier to keep the ambient temperature on the low side, but even if you aren't a health-freak keep chills at bay by making the most of those wool and cashmere throws, sheepskins and fake furs that adorn your sofas and chairs.

three summer coolers

1 • ceiling fan

It is possible to keep the air moving on airless days and sultry evenings with a large ceiling fan – the sort that conjures up images of past colonial elegance.

2 • sunscreens

Sun streaming through windows can turn a room into a sauna. Slatted and roller blinds, muslin screens or fine cotton curtains keep things under control. Or put a screen in front of a window.

3 • dress down

In warmer months, you could replace heavy curtains with lighter ones, or simply leave the window bare. You could also replace winter-weight cushion covers and throws with cotton and linen, or even follow the practice of well-ordered households of the past where sofas and chairs were dressed for summer in loose covers of light fabrics and chintzes (see 100).

hidden source 47

Sometimes it's possible to warm a room without it showing (or almost!)

underfloor heating

This is usually installed at the building stage as it involves incorporating hot water pipes or electrical elements into the solid floor. However, new developments and new products have made this form of heating more accessible, easier to install and more flexible so that you can choose to use it in just one room. It works extremely well with stone floors but it is now possible to use it under some wooden floors.

warm-air systems

These systems conduct warm air through metal or plastic-covered vents or grilles in walls or floors. The vents have very little visual impact but it is important to ensure that they remain unobstructed by furniture and furnishings.

long, low panel heaters

Placed at floor level these low heaters are very understated and, unlike standard radiators, will not take up valuable wall space. They can be part of either a hot-water fed or electrical heating system.

48

radiators with style

Radiators were once something you would try and disguise as much as possible, but those days are past. Now that designers have truly got to grips with them, they have come into their own. Some of these radiator ideas will be a stunning feature in your living room in their own right or, if you prefer, choose one of the options that will allow your radiator to fade into the background.

old-fashioned

The traditional cast-iron radiators as used in old houses, schools and other public and commercial buildings have become very popular and their generous proportions and functional appearance suit large spaces and contemporary interior styles. Originals can be found at architectural salvage yards but can be expensive and don't always work efficiently even after restoration. However, in response to popular demand, manufacturers have added similar styles in a variety of colours to their latest ranges.

glass

The idea of an invisible radiator seems too good to be true but modern technology means that you can now find radiators in glass that are discreet enough for even the most minimalist interior.

slimline

It is now possible to find slim, perfectly plain radiator and electric heating panels in white and a range of sizes, colours and finishes. They look chic and modern and will complement any style.

flights of fancy

Radiators don't have to be hidden or disguised, especially if you invest in one of the latest distinctive designs. These include curved lines, spirals and grids in a variety of finishes. Look out for brilliant coloured metallics, too.

bog standard

The standard radiator looks fine, is remarkably inexpensive and works very efficiently. Blend it into the background by painting it the same as the wall or make it stand out by painting it a contrast colour or striking pattern.

radiator covers and shelves

A shelf just above a radiator improves its efficiency and provides an opportunity for an extra display area. Radiator covers were popular additions to the 'English Country House' look but have become less fashionable in recent years. However, they do suit certain interior styles. Modern, plainer designs that use newer materials such as metal mesh ensure they are smart rather than fussy.

fires and fireplaces

More and more people are turning to real fires to provide comfort and a cosy atmosphere and are busy installing new fireplaces or unblocking those that were previously covered up when central heating became popular. Of course there is nothing like a real fire but it is not always possible, safe or legal to have one. If you are reinstating a previously unused fireplace get the chimney checked by a qualified chimney sweep who will advise on its safety, efficiency and suitability. The state of the actual fireplace must also be checked before use and damaged firebricks may need to be replaced. Flame-effect gas fires are a cleaner, easier alternative but they will also need a chimney or flue and, of course, should be installed professionally. These are now available in a number of unusual and innovative designs including stainless steel and 'flaming' ceramic 'pebbles'. Electrical flame-effect fires don't have real flames but don't need a chimney either. Even if you don't have a fire, a fireplace provides a focus for a room, which, especially in older properties, can look empty without one.

traditional

A traditional-style fireplace that is elegant and understated will look good in almost any style of living room: a beautiful but large fire surround can look wonderful in a small room if it is allowed to stand out as the main feature against plain walls and sparse furnishings; a large decorative fireplace can look stunning in a pared-down, modern interior; a small, pretty fireplace need not look lost in a large, opened-up space if it forms the focal point of a cosy seating arrangement.

modern

The 'hole in the wall' fireplace has no fire surround or mantelpiece and therefore looks suitably minimal and modern. This style looks particularly effective when the opening is sited above floor level and many designs for these include additional space for storage of logs or display. Contemporary flame-effect fires also work well in these simple openings. The current fashion for retro styles has revived the long, low fireplace with tiles or slate and an integrated seat such as used in the modern fifties houses.

stoves

Wood-burning or solid-fuel stoves come in a variety of designs from new, sleek stainless-steel models to antique, pretty French enamelled versions. They pump out comforting heat and though not normally used for cooking they often have a hot plate for boiling a kettle or warming up a pan of soup. They must be vented to the outside via a chimney or balanced flue. Gas and electric versions don't feel quite the same but they look quite convincing.

light up

Lighting should be high on your list of priorities at the planning stage and when choosing from the wide range of options now available, it is important to address practical considerations, such as electric circuitry and the structure of your home, as well as the more aesthetic considerations. There are a number of excellent and sophisticated lighting systems available, some of which will require professional installation. However, simpler and cheaper solutions can be equally effective and are readily available in DIY and department stores as well as specialist shops. A flexible and imaginative approach to lighting will make it easier to adapt your living room to different needs and roles.

activity report

Start by listing all the different activities that will be taking place in your living room (see 8) and make sure you plan things in order to have appropriate and adequate lighting for each.

are you getting enough?

Don't be afraid to use several light sources: a good track or downlight system is perfect for general illumination; remember task lighting for desks, and perhaps also fitted to the underside of cupboards or shelves; and don't forget separate light sources for a dining area and work areas and individual lights or a spotlight system for display.

mood swings

The flick of a switch can make the mess disappear and change the atmosphere from frenetic activity to leisurely lounging. It can also turn a bright, busy family room into a calm space for quieter, more intimate moments. Working with plenty of bright light makes you more efficient and is better for your eyesight and health in general, but a lower level of light will help you relax after a hard day.

in the spotlight

Highlight your good features. Track systems with halogen lights or spots offer the opportunity to light different areas at the same time as well as individual items. Uplights on walls or above cupboards look sophisticated, but simple clip-on lamps are effective and easy to use and can be moved around if you want to change the emphasis. Lighting inside cupboards will show off your collection to perfection.

the right direction

Correct positioning of lighting is very important so think carefully, or take advice. The centre of the ceiling may seem the obvious place for a track system but it could mean you end up standing between the light source and its target. Try to position work lights so they are in front of you.

circuit training

Always consult an electrician when installing a lighting system to ensure the lighting circuit is capable of powering the number and type of lights you want. Many track and downlight systems use low-voltage lights and need a transformer and a separate circuit. It is important not to overload a circuit. Using a bulb with too high a wattage can do this and can cause damage from overheating.

plug-ins

If the thought of new wiring puts you off, don't despair. There are plenty of lights that can be plugged into existing sockets. Wall-mounted or clip-on versions of desk lamps make good reading lights; table lamps provide intimacy; floor lamps and uplights can be used to define different areas; plug-in striplights or rows of downlights can be fixed under, on top of or inside cupboards, and beneath shelves.

pending

The days of a single light hanging in the middle of a room are past but pendant lights (there are plenty of good designs around) are useful and can look great. Hung low over tables they isolate and emphasise the area in an understated way. For extra versatility look for those with a rise and fall mechanism.

light fantastic

Make the most of the wonderful array of lighting now available. Chandeliers, fancy wall lights, fairy lights and even a flash of neon can give your living room extra sparkle and allow you to turn it into a more glamorous, chic or fun place to be.

wall light

Wall lights come in all shapes and sizes, from the traditional bracket light with pretty shades to smart designer versions in etched glass and even rubber. A new wall light concept comprises a row of lights, concealed under a shelf or behind a pelmet, which throw a subtle wash of background light across the wall.

10 ideas

wired-up 51

New interior projects inevitably require cabling for extra electric sockets and new lighting. If you are having structural work done this makes it easier to run the necessary wiring underneath the floor, in ceilings, through cavity walls or under new plaster. Now is the perfect opportunity to include additional wiring for sound systems, telephone, TV and Internet connections and perhaps to combine them all in an integrated system, which can be controlled from a single switch or console. For more modest alterations cables can be run along skirting boards and walls neatly and safely enclosed in plastic conduit (see 18).

what's hot? 52

standard lamps

Standard lamps are back. Look out for new straight bases topped with large drum shades in bright colours and bold geometric patterns.

coloured glass

Glass pebble and globe lamps are all the rage. They give a gentle glow and look great used in groups or placed on the floor in unexpected places.

rows

If you hate central ceiling lights but need the sort of overall illumination they provide, use longer flexes and hang rows of simple shaded lights above tables, worktops or desks.

53

lighting you never dreamed possible

twenty-four-hour day

Daylight bulbs give a whiter, brighter light similar to daylight that is easier on the eye and is generally thought to be healthier and of help in preventing SAD (Seasonal Affective Disorder), a suggested cause of winter depression. The down side is that the bulbs are more expensive and the quality of light is rather cold.

light show

If you fancy a bit of theatre then why not indulge in a system that enables you to control the lighting throughout the entire house by remote control. And it's not just a matter of on or off; you can adjust light levels and also change the colour to suit your mood.

floor show

Lights set into the ground are commonplace in public spaces and commercial building and are being installed in the smartest domestic interiors too. Put in a row to divide a space with a wall of light.

flooring matters

New floor treatments have had a great impact on our homes in recent years. There is a huge range of materials that are now easier to use and cheaper, which makes the task of installing a new floor much less daunting than it once was. Choice of floor covering is important to the look, but if you are considering stone, concrete or tiles, you must also take into account the suitability of the existing floor and the structure of your property.

When you are looking around, don't forget industrial and contract flooring products in carpet, rubber and vinyl. They are especially hardwearing and come in a number of unusual designs, finishes and colours including metallic. Although they are normally only sold in large quantities, you may be able to

5 ideas

negotiate smaller amounts through dealers. Look on the Internet.

appearance

Just as scruffy shoes will detract from even the most expensive outfit, so a less-than-perfect floor can completely spoil an otherwise perfect interior. Today's spacious, unified look is enhanced by large expanses of bare floor, but even if you don't have large spaces, the right flooring helps. Small rooms will feel bigger with a light-coloured floor, especially if it tones with the walls and furnishings and if you extend it to other parts of the house. The choice is wide so take time to find something that suits your chosen style. You never know, you may be so inspired by a flooring material that it becomes the star, and the basis for a whole new look!

feel

Provided there aren't too many gaps between the boards, wooden floors feel warm to the touch and also give a friendly feel and look to a room. Solid wooden floors are laid onto wooden joists and have a natural

spring, which is kind to feet and legs. Stone floors are wonderfully cool in hot weather but cold in winter, although under-floor heating can make them perfect all year round (see 47). Stone, concrete and tiles are mostly laid on a solid sub-floor and are therefore more tiring for long periods of standing. Carpet is soft and comforting, and natural floor coverings bridge the gap between carpet and wood, though they can be a little scratchy on bare skin.

sound

Sound will resonate around a room with bare floors and will spread to other areas. Solid wood will absorb a certain amount of sound and certainly more than stone or concrete, but ground-floor rooms will be less noisy as the earth will absorb some of the sound and vibration. Sound-reducing materials can be used under surfaces such as laminated wood to minimise noise problems. Carpet is also quiet to walk on and absorbs a lot of sound especially if used with a good underlay, which also helps keep out noise from below.

strength

Unless your property is in bad repair the floors should be strong enough for normal activity, but if you have very heavy furniture or plan to dance or do vigorous exercise, you should check that everything is in good order. Irresponsible removal of supporting walls, damp and wet or dry rot can all affect a floor's strength. In addition, check that floors are strong enough to support the weight if you want to choose a heavy flooring material.

practicality

Practical considerations can curb your aspirations. Pale tones may look sophisticated but they also show the dirt. Bare boards are great but they can be draughty, and little feet and knees can get splinters. Concrete and stone are fine until you drop your favourite plate, and tiles can turn into skating rinks when wet. Stains are more difficult to remove from carpet and natural floor coverings, and the cat can soon rough up a nice smooth carpet surface.

wooden floors

Wood is a common flooring material, either in the form of ordinary floorboards, often covered with carpet, linoleum or vinyl, or in the guise of wood block or thick planks that are intended to be left bare or used with rugs. There are plenty of new finishes on the market, too. Wooden floors are normally laid directly on to the joists after the removal of the old boards, but they can also be fixed to a wooden framework fixed to an existing solid floor such as concrete. For floors laid directly on to the ground, a damp-proof membrane must be placed underneath to stop damp and rot.

stain

Wood stains bring out the grain and add a characterful glow to the humble floorboard. Coloured versions are also available. Do a test in an inconspicuous area first as the results can be much darker than anticipated.

paint

Floor paint gives a flat, solid colour; for a gentler look use emulsion or one of the special decorator's floor paints and seal it with matt polyurethane varnish. If you want to be creative you could paint on stripes or chequerboard patterns.

oils and wax

Products such as linseed oil and Danish oil mellow the wood and help retain its character. Polished wax floors have a wonderful glow but will need re-waxing at regular intervals. Some wax products contain additives that increase stain resistance, but they can form a surface coating that looks unnatural and can be difficult to remove.

old floorboards

Freshen up old boards by sanding them (providing they are in good condition and don't have too many gaps), then sealing, staining or painting. Reclaimed boards give a sought-after aged look.

solid wood

The best new boards are thick with few knots and imperfections. Wide boards are more costly, but look it. New floors are often pre-finished: an oiled finish is the most natural but needs regular attention. Sealing makes the wood easier to keep clean and protects it from water damage.

laminated wood

Readily available and easy to lay, these floors are usually made from a thin layer of wood veneer glued to a composite board such as MDF, but beware of very cheap versions as they often have a plastic coating with a printed image of wood rather than the real thing. Can be laid on top of existing boards, concrete or any level surface – even carpet – and the surface is smooth and seam free.

plywood and chipboard

Chipboard panels, which fix together with a tongue-and-groove joint, are used in most new buildings as a base for other floor coverings but they can work on their own if they are stained, painted and sealed. For the rough and ready industrial look, use sheets of plywood or chipboard with a coating of clear sealant.

stone floors 56

Stone is a beautiful and hardwearing material that is very suitable for a living room and and gives a stunning effect. It is pleasantly cool in summer but can be cold in winter unless you have underfloor heating (see 47). It is now widely available and the new, thinner stone tiles and flexible adhesives make it easier to install. Though best laid on a concrete sub-floor, it can sometimes be laid on top of wood. The cost varies depending on quality: to the untrained eye one piece of stone may look much like another but an expert will be able to help you avoid expensive mistakes.

old stone

Old stone flags, with their uneven surface and evidence of wear, add a touch of history to any interior. If you have a stone floor but it is in poor condition or in the wrong place it is worth cleaning it up and re-laying it. Alternatively, buy old slabs from an architectural salvage company.

limestone

The pale tones and smooth, matt surface of limestone are perfect for today's simple yet sophisticated interiors. Pale cream is popular but it also comes in greys, deeper colours and randomly marked surfaces.

slate

Although slate comes in different colours it is most common in grey, which can vary from dark charcoal to whitish. The familiar 'cleft' surface looks rugged but slate is also available with a smooth surface for a sophisticated look.

marble

Marble is a hard form of limestone but normally has distinctive veining, which can vary from subtle to dramatic. The colours range from fresh-looking white with greys, greens and blues, to warmer pinks and beiges.

care of stone

Newly quarried stone oxidises over time to become harder and less porous. A new stone surface is normally treated once it has been installed using a sealer, which reduces porosity. Afterwards, regular washing with a neutral soap is what is needed to clean and feed the stone. Within a few years of use, the surface will become hard and stain-resistant and easy to maintain.

tiled floors

Tiles are hardwearing, easy to clean and very versatile and are now more widely used in living rooms.

ceramic floor tiles

Available in an enormous range of materials and shapes in shiny, matt or textured finishes, and in many sizes and thicknesses, colours and patterns – from plain white to wild patterns, as well as convincing imitations of stone. Glazed tiles reflect the light and can look cold: matt finishes have a subtler look.

quarry tiles

The distinctive reddish tones of quarry tiles look warm but can dominate, but they also come in black and beige. They are often laid in a chequerboard pattern.

terrazzo

Made by mixing ground or small pieces of stone with cement and pigments, terrazzo is best known for its distinctive speckly appearance, though it is also available in bright colours and plain finishes. It was once only laid as a slab but is now available as tiles, too. The surface is very robust and the tiles can be fixed with adhesive or set into a bed of sand and cement.

mosaic

These tiles are very chic especially in muted colours and a matt finish. They can look fussy so stick to plain colours with perhaps a discreet pattern around the edge.

stainless-steel tiles

Either plain or with a raised pattern, stainless-steel tiles look unusual, very industrial and very 21st-century.

concrete floors

Concrete looks good as a flooring in its own right, particularly in modern and industrial-style spaces. The standard grey colour can be varied with the addition of whiteners and pigments. Laying concrete is a skilled job to be undertaken by a professional who will also advise on concrete's suitability for your property and on the correct sub-floor. The sub-floor must be level and firm to prevent the slab cracking. It can take 28 days for a concrete floor to dry out and the surface must be sealed to prevent the release of dust, but if you want a more even finish, floor paint covers well and also acts as a seal.

covered up

59

Even though you may long for a beautiful bare solid wood or stone floor it is not always possible or practical. There are many advantages in covering up floors especially if they are in poor condition or if the work required to put down a solid floor is beyond your patience or your budget. Bare boards can look great but can also seem cold and unfriendly, while other poor-quality surfaces, such as old concrete, may be dusty and unhealthy. If you decide to cover up, remember that many floor coverings are relatively inexpensive, and rubber, vinyls and linoleum provide a good-looking, easy-care alternative to the traditional carpet. As you will see, the choice is wide and you are bound to be able to find a floor covering that suits your needs without having to compromise on style or colour.

three good reasons to cover a floor

1 • it's fashionable

Even the most ardent minimalists are covering their concrete with carpet and re-discovering the pleasures of being able to lie on the floor to watch TV. Linoleum and natural floor coverings such as coir have been popular for a while, in response to the demand for natural, eco-friendly materials. Hemp is one of the newest additions. Purists love the sophisticated, matt finish of rubber and though they may shudder at the thought of vinyl, they are taking an interest in new commercial vinyls, such as those with metallic finishes or photographic images.

2 • it's sensible

As already mentioned, it may be mandatory for people living in flats to have carpet (see 54), but even those in isolated mansions appreciate carpet's sound-absorbing properties and warmth. Bare, hard floors are not kind to children's heads and knees and resound to the clatter of plastic toys, so family life may be more harmonious on a soft surface. Many properties have floors that are meant to be covered: ordinary floorboards can be left bare but they don't keep out dust and draughts. And where floors are in poor condition, covering them is the sensible option. A well-laid fitted floor covering transforms a room and makes it look 'finished'.

3 • it's versatile

Opting for covered floors does not mean compromising your style preferences. The bare look is as much about keeping spaces un-cluttered as about the materials used. A plain, white rubber floor looks stunningly modern and a tight-weave coir or sisal has a similar look and feel to wood. Though you may be wary of 'imitations' there are some very convincing tile and stone finishes in good-quality vinyl, which doesn't require a solid sub-floor, can be laid directly onto boards, and because weight is not an issue, can be laid in an upstairs room. Linoleum is great for retro and modern but if subtle isn't your style you could opt for bright colours and jazzy patterns in vinyl. Carpet complements any style whether you go for plain restraint or the comfort of deep pile.

linoleum, rubber and vinyl

60

Although not always inexpensive, good quality linoleum, rubber and vinyl offer a floor surface in a variety of finishes that looks good and is easy to maintain.

linoleum

Made from natural materials including wood, flour, linseed oil, natural resins and pigments, which give even bright colours a muted quality, linoleum is an expensive material especially as professional fitting is crucial for a good finish. It can be cut and laid in any pattern.

rubber

Rubber gives the perfect smooth, matt, solid colour finish for the minimal look but it is expensive and marks easily. It is available in tiles and sheets in a large number of colours and also in raised patterns, such as dots. It is relatively expensive and will be more successful if laid by a professional.

vinyl

Good-quality vinyl flooring is hardwearing but expensive and is available in many designs, including faux terracotta, stone, marble or the Roman temple look. It comes in tiles and sheets and should be laid on a perfectly flat surface as imperfections will show and will wear easily. Cheap and cheerful vinyl tiles usually have an adhesive backing and are easy to lay. Avoid using vinyl in very large areas as joins can be unsightly, but if you invest in the highest quality it will be laid professionally and the joins won't show.

61 carpet

Fitted carpet is back in fashion. It is warm, comforting and quiet and is often a lot cheaper than other flooring options. It also comes in many colours and textures from inexpensive cord to thick shag pile. Wool is best as synthetics can look shiny and give you an electric shock. Use a good-quality underlay, even with inexpensive carpet, as it will help with wear and sound-proofing. Ribbed and corded designs are hardwearing and are good for places where there is a lot of passing traffic. Deep pile is luxurious but won't keep its looks if it is subjected to too many feet. Plain light colours will give your living room a sense of spaciousness, while dark colours will make it look smaller – and will show up dust and fluff. Patterned carpet can dominate but there are stripes and checks and geometric designs if you crave a bit of variety. Also watch out for the 'natural floor' look in wool or wool mixes (see 63). To be truly up-to-date, use industrial-quality cord with a contrasting border.

62 rugs

If you love bare floors but find them impractical or stark, you can have the best of both worlds by opting for rugs instead of fitted carpet. You will still enjoy the look and feel of a beautiful floor but noise will be reduced and comfort increased.

oriental carpets and rugs

The rich colours and patterns of oriental carpets never go out of fashion. The best are enormously expensive but some are more reasonable. If you are spending a lot, make sure you buy from a reputable retailer and do some research so you know what you are paying for. Woven dhurries and kelims come in a wide range of designs, mostly geometric, in rich vegetable dyes, but there are also plenty of plain or striped cheap and cheerful versions.

contemporary

Many designer/makers produce rugs that are almost artworks for the floor: keep an eye open at craft markets, studios and galleries. Modern furniture retailers sell similar pieces, usually in simple, abstract designs and bold colours.

flat woven

Influenced by the Scandinavian look, these neat woven wool rugs are a smart, Western version of the dhurry. Colours tend to be muted with greys, beiges and browns in plains, understated stripes and geometric designs.

furry and woolly

The furry rug, much admired in the seventies, is back. White is still the favourite but it gets grubby quickly so why not try one thrown over a chair or sofa? It will look just as good there.

tatami

These distinctive traditional Japanese mats are perfectly suited to a Zen-inspired interior. Made from natural fibres, they are large but light and quite thin. You could use several of them to cover up a floor that you are unable to change.

natural floor coverings 63

Sisal, coir, seagrass and jute are usually referred to as 'natural' floor coverings. Their warm, neutral colours and crunchy textures blend with most surroundings and look crisp and neat against pale or white walls. Hardwearing, they come in a variety of weaves, from plain flat weaves to bolder, hairy, herringbones. The coarse-textured fibres can feel scratchy, but some are finer and smoother. Coir, seagrass and hemp are reasonably soft.

It can be a problem keeping natural floor coverings looking good as stains are not easily removed and, although many are now pre-treated with a stain-resistant finish, any spills tend to stick between the fibres. The popularity of natural floor coverings has led many manufacturers to produce new products in wool, linen and cotton that retain the natural look but are softer and easier to maintain. These also include a greater variety of colours, including soft greens, blues and greys, indigos and reds, as well as stripes. Many designs are available as rugs, some with a border in a contrasting colour and some with a woven or printed pattern.

luxury extra

For the ultimate luxury floor covering – choose leather! Although it is extremely expensive it can look fabulous, particularly in a smartly contemporary living space. Leather is surprisingly hardwearing and mellows wonderfully with age.

wall sense: how to make your walls super-smooth

When you have stripped a wall ready for decorating a few lumps and bumps may remain. Don't worry too much as once you have painted or papered and added all the stuff that usually fills up a living space, even quite rough surfaces will go unnoticed. If, however, you are a perfectionist, you may want to make an extra effort to ensure a good finish.

5 ideas

fill

Fine cracks and small holes are easy to deal with. Fill them with good-quality filler (leaving the filler proud to allow for shrinkage when dry), then sand down with fine abrasive paper; repeat the process if necessary until all flaws have been obliterated.

re-plaster

Very poor, damaged wall surfaces with extensive areas of missing plaster should be re-plastered to achieve a good, even finish. Unless you are very competent, you must employ a professional plasterer, as plastering is a skilled job and should not be attempted by an amateur.

skim

If the plaster is too rough to fill, but not bad enough to need re-plastering, a thin skim coat of new plaster will provide a smooth surface. As with plastering, this needs the professional touch.

clad

For very rough surfaces or damaged walls, which cannot easily be plastered, consider having them re-clad with plasterboard (which is often finished with a skim coat) or wood panelling. This also provides the ideal opportunity for incorporating extra insulation.

line

If you don't want the bother and mess of plastering or skimming, you could fill in the cracks and holes and then use a lining paper to give a uniform surface for painting or papering. Hang the paper horizontally to lessen the likelihood of subsequent layers of paper pulling the liner away from the wall and if you are painting on top, the lines won't be so obvious.

three wall finishes

1 • bare plaster

We now appreciate age and wear in old houses and often leave characterful damaged and worn surfaces as a feature. In some old houses the even finish of new paint does not blend in well whereas bare plaster does, though modern plaster is usually a pink colour that does not always suit an old building. If this is the case, you can get it in a traditional grey, so ask your plasterer to investigate. Whether it is old or new, plaster is dusty so you should have it sealed.

2 • trendy paint

The dry, matt finishes of distempers and dead-flat paints are designed to complement older properties but also look modern and sophisticated in new and unremarkable buildings.

3 • wood

Wood panelling varies from the elegant panels of 18th-century houses to the tongue-and-groove of more modest dwellings. Lining the walls with plain veneered-wood panels was popular in the seventies and has become so again. Plywood and even chipboard can also be used if you like the industrial look.

touch the ceiling

65

Ceilings should be washed down and filled in the same way as walls, but damaged surfaces may need professional attention as they are more difficult to deal with, and more prone to falling down.

treatment

Ceilings often get ignored and painted white out of habit, particularly in the living room where other features are used to bring in the colour and texture. Light colours make a ceiling rise while dark ones will lower it, so you can use this knowledge to pull a room into shape. Painting the ceiling the same colour as the walls looks more harmonious and will help play down any imperfections. If you want to make a feature of your ceiling, you could try painting it a bright or very dark colour or even using a printed wallpaper.

mouldings

Keeping original mouldings will retain the character of your home and will not look out of place in a very modern interior scheme. They are best painted the same colour as the ceiling or, if the ceiling is colourful, white or a pale neutral. If the pattern has lost definition by being covered with many coats of paint, you can remove the paint by using a special paste. Alternatively, you can just wash it down, using a washing-up brush or similar to get into the nooks and crannies, then paint it again. Perfect mouldings will retain their definition if spray-painted – distemper is good for this.

textured ceilings

If you have a textured plaster finish on your ceiling, you either have to choose to love it or get it re-plastered. If you want to add texture to a ceiling there are plenty of embossed papers to choose from. A very damaged or uneven surface could be covered with tongue-and-groove boarding for a cosy cottage feel.

paint 66

Paint is now available in an ever-increasing choice of colours and a wide variety of types and finishes, including a number of specialist paints based on historically correct recipes and colours. Don't limit paint to walls, ceilings and paintwork: it also looks great on floors and furniture and is an easy way to transform a dull sitting room into an exciting living space. The demand for paint that is easy to apply, quick-drying and environmentally friendly has led to the development of more water-based products that are non-toxic and low-odour. Before buying and using paint, always read the instructions on the tin.

emulsion

Emulsion comes in a matt or slightly shiny 'silk' finish in a huge number of colours. It is water-based but may have additives such as vinyl to give a more durable, wipe-down surface. Easy to apply, some emulsion paints will cover in one coat but two or even three may be better.

gloss

Gloss is shiny and tough and is suitable for woodwork but can also be used on walls. Solvent-based gloss is more hardwearing but more difficult to apply, and brushes and splashes must be cleaned with white spirit. Water-based gloss is easier to use, more environmentally friendly and is better for walls.

eggshell

Used for woodwork and occasionally walls, eggshell has a slightly reflective quality. Water-based versions are quick drying but not as hardwearing as solvent-based ones and may need extra coats.

floor paint

Specially formulated for a durable surface this usually has a low-sheen finish. Originally available in a limited range of colours it is now offered in a wide range and is often included in specialist and designer paint collections.

specialist paints

• distemper: a traditional paint with a chalky finish, it looks wonderful in older properties and brings character to new ones, but the surface is unstable and rubs off. Produced in limited ranges of 'authentic' colours.

• limewash: a traditional paint with a matt finish, but less powdery than distemper. It allows walls to breathe, which makes it good for new plaster and old properties.

• flat or dead flat oil: oil-based paint with a perfectly matt finish suitable for woodwork and walls.

• stencils: the new way to use stencils is boldly, all over the wall in large patterns. They work best if the wall and the stencil colours are similar in tone or character.

67

wall coverings

Wallpapers are making a comeback and in a huge variety of styles.

wallpaper

• Printed wallpaper, especially the new designer ranges and hand-blocked historical styles, is in all the trendiest homes. Look out for vintage papers in antique markets and specialist shops.

• Textured papers range from heavily embossed to modern geometric designs and the ubiquitous woodchip. Should be painted.

• Many of the latest wallpapers come ready pasted. They are coated with an adhesive that is activated by dipping in cold water in a specially designed trough.

paper-backed fabric

This offers a foolproof way of putting fabric on your walls. Hessian is making a comeback but silks and damasks are also available. If you are planning on using a special, expensive fabric, employ a professional to hang it from battens.

68

one wall – five ideas

pattern

Confined to one wall, a piece of rare retro or hand-blocked, wildly expensive paper becomes affordable and won't overwhelm the room.

colour

A single wall of bold, painted colour can bring a room to life.

wood panelling

One wall of dark, distinctively grained wood panelling will add drama to your living room, while on all four walls it will just look gloomy.

the big picture

Have a favourite photo blown up to whole wall size and printed on wallpaper by a specialist company.

display

Gather your favourite treasures and collections into one spectacular display either hung on the wall, arranged on shelves or in glass-fronted cupboards and display cases.

69 windows

The ever-expanding variety of products and ideas gives us more scope for our window treatments than ever before. Recent interior fashions favour simple window coverings such as blinds and fabric panels, or the option of leaving the window bare in order to appreciate the light, a great view, or the window itself. Or you can use opulent fabrics and fittings if you prefer, which may be best if you want a cosier feel. It is important to consider privacy, too, but you can always retain the simplicity of plain blinds, or a combination of blinds and curtains, and still have the flexibility of providing privacy and ambience at the pull of a cord or the swish of a curtain.

keeping up appearances

Windows have a huge impact on both the exterior and interior of a property and are an important element in any design scheme. Keep the frames in good decorative order and don't forget to enhance your carefully considered window treatments or coverings by making the effort to keep the glass sparkling clean both inside and out.

private life

Even if we enjoy looking into other people's living rooms we don't necessarily like the idea of passers-by looking in on us. This used to mean net curtains that could provide privacy while maintaining light levels, but there are plenty of other options from blinds to old linen tea towels. It isn't always necessary to cover the whole window; covering just the lower half is often enough to allow privacy while still letting in light and a bit of a view.

10 ideas

private view

Even a dismal back yard has the odd visit from a bird so there is usually something worth seeing through a window. Don't cut yourself off completely from the outside world: it can feel claustrophobic and make you feel quite anxious if you can't see out. It is surprising how much you can see in daylight through a fine cotton curtain or a slatted blind.

bare all

If you are not overlooked (or don't mind being watched) you may wish to leave your windows completely bare, but as the window frame will be very much on show make sure it is well painted and in good repair. If you do need a little privacy and the view isn't great, use etched glass in the whole of the window, or just in the lower half. If you don't want to go to the trouble and expense of getting new glass it is possible to buy adhesive film or spray-on glass-etch products from craft shops. Placing a screen in front of a window allows you to go bare without impeding the light too much.

lighten up

Nowadays we like to get as much light into our rooms as possible. Coverings and fittings can encroach on the glass area even when open so try to keep them well clear of the frame. Fit poles and tracks so that the curtains can be pulled right back at the sides and, if possible, keep them well above the frame at the top. Remember that slatted and roman blinds will still take up room when pulled up so set them high to keep them out of the way.

replacement windows

Insensitive window replacements are very common and as well as looking unattractive can also reduce the value of a property, so it may be worth investing in new frames in a style and material more fitting to your home. New glass doors and windows used as part of improvements or new building works can transform the living space especially if it opens onto a garden or roof terrace.

cover-up

Not all windows are beautiful and if they threaten to spoil your living room look, you can cover them up in ways that don't cut out too much light. A plain curtain or panel of translucent fabric is the simplest solution, but slatted blinds that are wider and longer than the window are effective, too. Made-to-measure shutters or plantation blinds hide a multitude of sins but for a harder-edged, modern look you could screen the whole window using acrylic sheet, etched glass, steel mesh or even paper. Fix these directly to the window frame, hinge them like shutters, or attach them to a sliding track.

glazed over

Double-glazing is great for keeping out draughts, dirt and noise but a hermetically sealed environment can cause condensation. Good-quality double-glazed windows look as good as single-glazed windows but some cheaper versions (and secondary glazing with a separate second layer of glass) is less aesthetically pleasing and can be difficult to clean.

awkward shapes

Not all windows are conveniently square or in a position that makes it easy to have a curtain rail or blind. Arched, round or Gothic-shaped windows are best left bare but if privacy is an issue, use etched glass, hang simple, plain curtains from a rail fixed well above the window, or invest in made-to-measure shutters.

safe house

Windows play an important role in security so it makes sense to keep them in good repair. Some insurance policies necessitate the installation of window locks but remember to keep the keys accessible (but not to burglars) as locking yourself in could be dangerous in an emergency.

blind devotion

70

Blinds look less fussy than curtains and suit the pared-down look of many contemporary living spaces. Formerly an expensive made-to-measure option, their popularity has seen an enormous rise thanks to the number of off-the-shelf versions. These are available in a wide selection of styles and sizes, from simple, inexpensive roll-up reed to the popular wooden slatted variety. They will not detract from the good points of a window but can be used to disguise its bad ones. Blinds can blend discreetly into the background, sharpen up a modern living room or be used as a contrasting feature.

cotton rug

Instead of a fabric Roman blind use a colourful cotton or wool dhurry or kelim-style rug. Fix it to a batten at the top of the window and allow the fringed end to fold over at the front; sew on rings and thread strings through (just as with Roman or Swedish blinds) so that you can pull it up and let it down. The weight of the rug is enough to ensure it hangs well.

coloured slats

We have got hung up on mostly white or wooden blinds but you can get made-to-measure and ready-made slatted blinds in a wide range of colours. Baby blue or pink suit a fifties retro look.

duo

If standard size blinds are too short for your window use two, one hung from the top and the other fixed half way down or along the line of a glazing bar. You could also use two different types of blind: for example, a slatted blind at the bottom and a roller blind at the top. The lower blind can be left down to give privacy without keeping out all the light.

paper

Go Japanese with paper blinds. They are light and easy to hang from a couple of hooks or nails. They are often very inexpensive and therefore cheap to replace when they become torn or grubby. Why not experiment and make your own using some of the amazing hand-made or unusual papers available from specialist retailers or art shops?

roman splendour

Indulge in luxury Roman blinds in an extravagantly beautiful fabric and line them with velvet or silk. Instead of getting hung up on neat tailoring, make them big and baggy. This looks great in coarse linen or flannel lined with ticking, printed silk or cotton.

shutter ways

Shutters are increasing in popularity as a window covering. As well as folding back to leave the window fashionably bare, they can also be positioned to provide shade in harsh sunlight. Styles vary from the elegant panels of 18th-century houses to modern, perfectly plain designs, which will have minimal impact on a minimal interior. To make sure they fit properly, shutters should be made-to-measure and installed by a professional carpenter. Louvred plantation shutters can be adjusted to act like blinds and allow light in during the day. They are expensive but are a good investment. Other variations on the shutter include lengths of muslin stretched between portière rods, to act as a sun and insect screen.

off-the-peg

Sometimes ready-made kitchen or wardrobe doors are the right size for your windows, so why not use them as smart, co-ordinating shutters.

found objects

If you like the distressed look, use old planks of wood or doors complete with worn and peeling paint in place of more usual shutters.

smart and smooth

Acrylic sheet, available in a variety of opaque or translucent colours, is a chic alternative but is tricky to cut so get that done professionally.

curtains

Curtains soften the look of a room and make it more intimate and cosy by night, which is essential when it comes to living spaces. There will always be a place for beautifully made, fully lined curtains but don't be afraid to adopt a more casual approach if that's what you prefer. However, if a bit of fuss is to your taste, have a look at the wonderful trimmings on the market. These range from stiff organza ribbons to over-the-the top tassels. Any of these would add a touch of extravagance.

straight up and down

Simple, ungathered panels suit simple, uncluttered interiors. They are easy to make, require less fabric than gathered curtains and look best hung from poles, rings or eyelets. Plain linens, cottons and wools are good for a restrained effect, but for something different you could use an exotic embroidered panel or a unique length of vintage fabric. For a touch of variety, add a coloured border or a contrasting panel at the bottom in a print or heavier fabric.

quilted

Padded or quilted curtains are great draught excluders especially if you have them extra long so that they fold on to the floor. Use two layers of a light fabric with lightweight padding sandwiched in between for a look that's fluffy rather than heavy. An instant, but weightier alternative curtain is a ready-made quilt hung from a stout pole.

full works

If you love extravagance go for the full works with pencil pleats, pelmets and even tie backs. Velvet or silk are classic and floral prints are tempting, but why not consider curtains in smooth wool or smart pin-stripe suiting lined in coloured silk? Make them look sophisticated by keeping colours neutral or the same colour as the wall.

ready-made

The range of ready-made curtains is now pretty comprehensive and they are great because you just take them home and hang them up. Different headings are available including eyelets and loops. Use your imagination and look at other ready-made options such as blankets, fleecy and knitted throws or old linen sheets, which can be either made up into curtains or just draped over a pole.

new lengths

It is always tricky to get curtains to skim a floor or a windowsill exactly, so the new, relaxed approach to length can only be good news. The cropped look hangs well below a windowsill but doesn't reach the floor, and full-length curtains look more dramatic if they are allowed to crumple into a heap at the bottom. Even if you don't have full-length windows, curtains that hang from ceiling to floor will make a room look taller. Half-length, ungathered lengths of plain cotton or linen hung with clips or eyelets on a rod or wire are decidedly chic.

curtain fixtures and fittings

73

poles

Poles are available in a wide range of lengths, thickness and finishes. Materials include dull and shiny metal, pale or dark wood and painted finishes including gilt. Although the simplicity of these poles makes them perfect for today's fashions, they can be dressed up with decorative finials if you wish. If you fancy something a bit different look in builders' merchants and DIY stores for galvanised piping, wrought iron, dowelling or even broom handles. Poles are normally hung on brackets and the ends are finished with a finial to stop the curtains sliding off, but where the pole spans the whole length between two walls it can be slotted into special brackets fixed either side.

Curtains are hung from rings and hooks threaded onto the poles and these are normally sold alongside the poles, brackets and finials. Double brackets, which carry two poles of different weight, are also available and are a neat way of hanging two sets of window covering, one of which is normally a light sheer.

wires and cables

Wires and cables are perfect for the minimal look. Lightweight curtains and panels can be hung from them using eyelets, rings or clips. The cable is stretched between hooks or brackets and held taut using tensioners, which either come as part of a kit or can be bought from a DIY store.

rails

Traditional curtain rails come in a wide range of choices from simple plastic track, which is fine for straight runs and light curtains, to high-quality systems that include pull cords and extra tracks for a second set of curtains. It is worth getting them made-to-measure for the bends and curves of bay windows. There is normally one track per curtain, allowing the curtains to overlap when closed. This looks neat and eliminates any draughts. Look for smart new rails in which

the gliders are hidden behind a plain metal strip or inside metal tubing.

rings and things

There are many ways in which curtains can be attached to poles and tracks.

rings: currently the most popular, these are available to match the various poles, but you can use cheaper, or plainer alternatives such as old-fashioned curtain rings or perhaps a set of wooden or ornate metal ones picked up in an antique market. Rings either have a smaller ring for carrying the hook attached to the curtain heading, or are sewn directly onto the curtain. Some incorporate a clip for hanging lightweight fabrics.

eyelets: a crisp and modern choice, especially when used with plain cottons, linens and denim. They are now available in a variety of sizes, including very large, and in shiny and dull finishes, and though many come in kits for you to attach yourself, many more ready-made curtains now come with eyelets. The eyelets are threaded onto a pole or wire – but make sure they are big enough to allow the curtains to move freely.

tabs and loops: these can either be in the same fabric as the curtain or in a contrasting fabric or even in leather. A fancy bow can make a pretty addition. Tabs and loops need no extra hooks or rings as they thread directly on to a pole. They look neat and understated but are more suited to window coverings that are not pulled back. Loops that tie on to a pole or wire are easier to install.

74 fabric choices

Just as new interiors have become simpler and calmer so have fabrics. This doesn't mean that there aren't some wild and sumptuous materials around, but they are being used more discriminately. With many people opting for upholstery, blinds and curtains that blend with the living room rather than stand out, plain fabrics are more popular, but there are plenty of patterns, weaves and finishes to add texture and variety. Although many of the more sophisticated fabrics are very expensive there are plenty of less costly options that have the right feel and look for a modern, fresh design style. Look for coarse, loose-weave linen, denim and fresh cotton seersucker, or for a heavier feel, consider tweed. Although old lace curtains suit a romantic interior, there is a wide range of other translucent fabrics that provide colour, texture, pattern or simple restrained good taste for any style of living space.

natural selection

Enjoy the neutral subtle tones of natural fibres.
- unbleached cottons, coarse linens
- slubby cottons, wild silks
- crunchy textures, loose weaves
- felted wool, hessian

opulence

Indulge in rich colours and glorious patterns.
- soft velvets, dévoré
- silk damasks
- shot silk
- glazed chintz
- coloured organza, embroideries

pattern

Use sparingly or go for bold, but keep control of the colours.
- spriggy printed cottons
- toile de Jouy
- large florals
- checks, stripes, big spots
- bright abstracts

vintage

Turn bargains into chic while you indulge a passion for the past.
- antique lace
- faded velvet
- old bed and table linens
- original retro prints

smart

Use to bring discipline and elegance to a stylish living room.
- moleskin
- felt, flannel
- pinstripe suitings
- cotton twill
- heavy silk

casual

Relax with the comfort of fabrics you would also choose to wear.
- denim
- brushed cotton
- knits
- fleece
- tweed

soft options

To keep out prying eyes or unattractive views.
- muslins
- sari fabrics
- crisp, fine cotton
- organza, organdie
- heavy cotton lace
- self-coloured woven stripes and checks

75

what to look for when you buy
furniture frenzy

Buying furniture can be exhausting and confusing, so don't rush it. Explore all the possibilities by consulting magazines and catalogues and visiting a range of shops from the very posh to the very cheap. For older furniture, scour antique markets, house-clearances and junk shops, and check out salerooms and skips. Your budget may curb your enthusiasm but don't be afraid to buy fewer expensive but beautiful pieces – remember less can be more!

style

Don't feel you have to stick rigidly to a single style. Mixing is fashionable and even if you love ultra-modern, a good antique can look stunning. Similarly, simple modern shapes hold their own in a traditional setting.

function

Don't be swayed by looks. A chair or sofa may look sensational but loses its charm if it isn't comfortable. Check what you buy is suited to its purpose.

quality

Expensive doesn't necessarily indicate quality: you are sometimes paying for fashion. So examine before you buy, to check the materials and workmanship. And don't forget that inexpensive may mean inferior, but can still be good value for money.

size

Don't buy until you have checked the measurements and know a piece will fit. Scale is also important: pieces will work well together if their proportions are similar.

sell-by date

It is easy to be seduced by fashion, but stick to simple shapes and avoid trendy colours or quirky details. But don't be dull. Make your fashion statement with clever accessories in the latest colours, fabrics and designs.

keep or throw out?

When it comes to deciding if you should keep a piece of furniture, the heart can often rule the head. Asking yourself these questions can help.

do you like it?

You may like a piece of furniture for its familiarity but now's the time to be objective. Do you really like it for itself? If you do, you'll find a place for it – or perhaps even design your new living room around it.

does it fit in?

An item of furniture can be perfectly nice but sometimes it just doesn't pass the style check. Unless it does, get rid of it.

do you need it?

If a piece of furniture makes a room look cluttered or has been superseded by newer purchases, pass it on to a friend.

is it comfortable?

A comfortable chair or sofa should not be discarded lightly. If it is in very poor condition then bin it, but if it can be rehabilitated, it may be worth giving it a second chance.

is it useful?

If space is short, throw out any furniture that isn't used regularly or doesn't work well.

making the most of what you've got

It is not always possible, or desirable, to replace the furniture you have with something new, so why not try to see it in a new light (see 44)?

five ideas for making the best of things

1 • A random collection of dining chairs can be turned into a smart set with a coat of paint in a single colour or range of similar shades.

2 • Different styles of armchairs and sofas will look better covered in toning colours.

3 • New covers in a fashionable fabric will update an unfashionable chair or sofa, especially if you add a scattering of new cushions and throws.

4 • Sometimes a good clean is revealing. For example, wood will enjoy being stripped of old paint and varnish and fed with nourishing oils.

5 • Cover a battered old sofa with a huge fluffy wool rug and enjoy.

relax into this

Good-quality upholstery is an expensive but worthwhile investment so it is wise to do your homework before you buy. Prices range from very reasonable to decidedly expensive and on the whole the price reflects the quality of materials and construction. Cheap foam upholstery is fine but has a limited lifespan and is not usually robust enough to withstand heavy wear. More expensive sofas and armchairs are solidly made with high-quality upholstery materials attached to a sturdy frame, and feather rather than foam cushions.

three important considerations when buying a sofa

1 • access

Narrow doorways, staircases and awkward corners can make it impossible to get a sofa or armchair into a room. A good retailer will offer to do an access check and if there is a problem, may suggest an alternative, such as getting the piece in via a window.

2 • price

Upholstery is often made up in the fabric of your choice, the cost of which is normally added to the listed price: make sure you are aware of the total cost when ordering.

3 • fire regulations

All fabrics specified for covering ready-made and made-to-order upholstery are subject to strict regulations concerning flammability. If you are supplying your own fabric make sure it complies: you will probably be asked to offer a certificate of proof.

five sofas to go

1 • Classic shapes such as the Chesterfield can have either a fixed seat or loose seat cushions. Button-backed versions are traditional but unbuttoned look more contemporary.

2 • Modern sofas are long and low in square or sensuously curved shapes. Fixed, or large, boxy cushions help ensure they look sleek and well-groomed, and slender metal or wooden legs keep them looking light.

3 • Rattan suggests sunshine and an outdoor ambience. Less expensive than upholstered furniture, it is not as hardwearing. Choose curvy styles that don't scratch or dig in to the backs of your legs and invest in good-quality cushions. Rattan's colour mellows and deepens with age.

4 • The Knole sofa, with its high back and arms tied together makes an effective draught excluder. Though traditionally upholstered in heavy fabrics, it can look great in plain cotton or brightly coloured velvet. For a lighter, more decorative look choose an elegant 17th- or 18th-century English or French sofa or chaise longue in rich silk or white linen.

5 • One of the most popular historical references is Art Deco but if you cannot find the genuine article there are several modern interpretations. The fashion for nostalgia also means that the classic three-piece suites of the thirties and forties are in demand as is the 'contemporary' furniture of the fifties with its spindly, splayed legs. Look in second-hand shops and specialist retro retailers.

three chairs for life

1 • Huge armchairs are perfect for curling up in and take up less space than a sofa. Old armchairs are particularly nice, especially in faded chintz or battered leather, but new, modern versions are also available.

2 • Partly upholstered chairs are smaller than the fully upholstered variety, which makes them suitable for small rooms. Look for Art Deco styles with curved wooden arms or modern interpretations with brushed aluminium or stainless-steel frames.

3 • The curvy club chair in traditional leather has recently made its way into many living rooms, but it also comes in modern squared-off shapes.

the footstool story

Footstools are back. Modern shapes look chic or jolly, depending on the fabric, while the traditional curvy-legged version is still one of the best. Footstools incorporating storage are very useful, while the long low ones can double as tables and look good in leather or suede.

sofa beds

For small or crowded homes where a guest bedroom is not an option a sofa bed is the perfect solution. There is now a wide range of styles and conformations available, making them easy to integrate into any decorative scheme.

pull-out traditional

This looks like a normal sofa. The classic sofa bed has a sprung frame folded inside the seat, which makes it more expensive than a standard sofa. Other versions of sofa beds have seat cushions that fold down to form a mattress on the floor (which may be difficult for older people to use). Unless you have a clear space in front of the sofa you may have to move things to open it out.

daybed

Daybeds are popular for daytime use but the larger ones are long enough to lie on full length, so the only thing you need to turn them into a bed is bedding. Designs vary from the perfectly plain cushion/mattress on a simple metal frame, to variations on

the chaise longue with a back and single arm. On the shorter versions the arms fold down to form the bed.

futon

The traditional Japanese futon mattress can be folded on to a variety of frames and bases and can be used as seating during the day. There are many variations on the theme, but the frames take up quite a lot of room and as the mattress is heavy, it can require quite a lot of effort to convert the futon into bed mode. Lighter, modern, versions fold down easily but as they are the length of a bed, they are larger than many sofas. A roll-up futon is another option but you will need to find somewhere to store it.

floor cushions

For informal visits or unplanned overnight stays, guests may be quite happy to bed down on large floor cushions (see 80). You can get box-shaped and futon cushions, which are more firm.

airbed

A deflated airbed takes up very little space and to save your breath they come with electric motors, which plug into an ordinary socket and inflate the bed in minutes.

comfortable touches

An easy way to update or lift a room is to add new cushions and throws in the latest fashionable colours and materials. Cushions can also make old, or badly designed furniture more comfortable and a few throws will cover up less-than-perfect, or outdated upholstery.

cushion news

• Scatter cushions come in a vast range of sizes, fabrics and designs. Take care when you buy, though. Too many of the same colour will look dull and too many different ones will look messy. Good-quality feather or fibre-filled are best.

• There are fabulous cushion covers around, including fine, ribbed, chunky and cable knits, some with buttons; fake fur – the hairier the better; fleece and sheepskin – real or fake; leather and suede; embroidered silks, tapestry, Indian fabrics, pleated

• Floor cushions are great for lolling around on or as impromptu beds. Being big they make an impact, so choose covers that minimise unless you want to make them a feature.

five throws

1 • cashmere – light, warm and luxurious

2 • woollen blanket – checks and prints, or reversible with leather-bound edges

3 • kelim-style – colourful

4 • ethnic – embroidered or boldly patterned bedspreads or panels

5 • shawls – fringed silk for romance, wool for comfort

tables etc

Whether you need somewhere to put your coffee and newspaper or a place to put a vase of flowers there is sure to be an occasional table to suit the job, and the look, of your living room.

long and low

The classic shape for coffee tables is also perfect for magazines – and even your feet. You often want a table in front of a sofa so make sure that it is high enough off the ground to allow you to stretch your legs out while seated, and make sure there is room to walk round it.

nesting

The space-saving nest of tables is great for snack time or unexpected visitors. New looks include bent plywood and simple shapes in solid wood.

storing

A table with a shelf for newspapers or magazines enables you to tidy up in a hurry but it can also be a good place to keep games or chocolates. Some new designs include provision for storing books or housing the 'drinks cabinet'.

displaying

A low table with a drawer beneath a glass top provides a great display opportunity for anything from photographs to a collection of cigar boxes. A console table or sideboard is the perfect height for flowers and a few carefully arranged objects.

wheeling and dealing

Sometimes tables are needed in different places at different times for different uses, so a set of wheels is a great asset. Trolleys are also useful for teatime dainties and serious cocktails, or as moveable storage for books and magazines.

five table looks

1 • glass top on polished aluminium or stainless-steel legs
2 • curved one-piece plywood
3 • chunky wood with a zinc-wrapped top
4 • low upholstered footstool
5 • raw wood with burrs and even holes

eating arrangements

Sitting round a table in comfort encourages conviviality among family and friends You of course need a table and chairs, but they don't have to match. An antique dining table can look stunning with modern chairs, while mismatched old chairs can be pulled together round a plain modern table. For originality, use quality garden furniture indoors or a cheap picnic bench painted with white gloss. Other possibilities are slick American-diner or minimal Japanese-teahouse styles.

five dining tables

1 • If you only use your living room occasionally for formal dining or entertaining, a folding or extending table is ideal. Tables can be extended with slot-in or pull-out leaves or their hinged sections can be unfolded. Tables that are still useable when folded are the most useful and look less makeshift. Look for circular tops that fold in half, square tops that

become rectangles and long narrow ones that fold lengthwise to become console tables.

2 • An oval table is elegant and takes up less room than a square or rectangular one. If the standard table is too wide, try a long narrow refectory style or a breakfast bar fixed to the wall. In a really tight space a gate-leg table can be placed against a wall or there are even tables that fold down from the wall.

3 • The glass-topped dining table is often seen as the epitome of modern furniture design. Some consist of a sheet of clear glass atop steel or wooden legs, but others have the glass set into a wooden or metal frame. They look wonderful but need a lot of care to keep them sparkling clean, and even though they are made of toughened glass, safety

is a consideration, especially in a home with young children or boisterous dogs.

4 • Even if your home is uncompromisingly modern, an elegant polished mahogany or rosewood antique table and chairs will never look out of place. Alternatively, plainer styles such as old refectory or school tables or traditional oak or pine kitchen tables will fit in with most styles and add an air of comfort.

5 • A wipe-clean surface is useful for a dining table, and there are plenty of plain laminated tables to choose from. Look out for curved plywood on splayed tubular steel legs or colourful, fifties-style laminate kitchen tables, sometimes with a steel edging. For a modern look the latest designer shapes are curvy in moulded plastic.

five dining chairs

1 • Sitting round a table is a lot more enjoyable if the chairs are comfortable: upholstered dining chairs encourage lingering over meals. Choose with or without arms, loose or fixed covers. Fully upholstered tub chairs are a real luxury but take up a lot of room.

2 • Sleek, modern chairs favour slender frames and legs in metal or wood, and seats in curved plywood, plastic or metal. Or if you prefer, there is a return to the slightly heavier wood Scandinavian-influenced designs of the sixties and seventies, with curved legs and backs.

3 • Bargains can still be found in chairs from old churches, schools and offices and fifties curved wooden chairs. More grown-up antiques – from Shaker to Queen Anne – are costlier, but keep an eye on sale rooms and the local paper (or cultivate a friendly antiques dealer).

4 • Folding or stackable chairs range from the cheap and cheerful wooden fold-up (try hanging these on the wall when not in use) to the modern stacking classic with curved ply seat. All are great space-savers.

5 • Benches look neater and more minimal and take up less space than chairs. They are perfect for the pared-down look as there is no jumble of chair backs and legs. Benches are also versatile: if everyone squashes up you can usually find room for one more guest. However, access can be awkward especially if the bench is against a wall. Look for smart benches in carved oak or more utilitarian styles in metal and laminate.

a word about sideboards

Sideboards are back in fashion though modern ones are more likely to house CDs, magazines and sound systems than the best china. The long, low sideboards on legs, typical of the sixties and seventies and currently very fashionable, were usually in richly coloured woods, often with a distinctive grain. They matched the dining table and chairs and it is still sometimes possible to find complete sets. New designs are influenced by this era but they also come in pale wood, and some have etched-glass doors. Older styles of sideboards – often called chiffoniers or buffets – are often ornate, high-backed affairs, sometimes with mirrors. They are big, solid and imposing, but provide plenty of storage space.

work plans desks and surfaces

Now that a large proportion of the population has a computer and an increasing number of people work from home, most furniture retailers offer 'home office' ranges that are designed to look good in a domestic setting. In addition, the popularity of the industrial, utilitarian look has made filing cabinets and office furniture very fashionable. All this means that you can have an attractive workspace in your living room if you wish, but there's no need to stick to office furniture: dining tables, bookshelves, cupboards and chests of drawers make good desks and storage and will help a work area to blend into the background.

desks to die for

• The classic roll-top desk with pigeon holes and drawers will inspire you to be organised and pay the bills on time.

• You could find a modern version of the huge metal thirties newspaper-office desk with lots of drawers. Get yourself an eyeshade and pretend you have a front page to hold.

• Small, elegant antique writing desks are perfect for reviving the art of letter writing or for starting that novel.

• It has become a classic, but a worktop resting on two or more filing cabinets makes a great desk. Choose brightly coloured or ultra-smart cabinets and a solid wood or glass top, and the ensemble will bring a chic quality to your living room.

• A beautiful dining table – any size, antique or modern, round or square – makes a stylish, minimal desk or can be called upon as a dining table when necessary.

• Try placing an old and beautiful or stylishly modern desk on its own, at a window or away from a wall, facing into the room. It will not only look nicer but will give you a better view when you're sitting at it.

84

a home for the computer

Computers have mostly had a positive impact on our lives but unfortunately they often have a less positive impact on our living rooms. If you have a modish flat-screen model in white or a chic colour, treat it as a stylish accessory and leave it on show, but if you have the grey box variety, you may want to conceal it when it is not in use. You must also consider the need for space around the computer for work-related paperwork and so on, not to mention printers and scanners. And even the best designs involve a potential tangle of cables. Keep these accessible but out of sight (see 18, 85).

computer table

If choosing a purpose-designed computer table, invest in one that looks good. There are models in etched glass and metal, graceful moulded plastic or curvaceous plywood. Some have wheels so you can move them to a more discreet location when not in use.

behind a wall

Use a dividing wall, either full- or half-height, to hide the computer (see 30, 31). The simplest consists of a panel of wood or laminate fixed to the back of a desk. Or opt for a sliding wall or panel to cover the work area completely.

in a cupboard

Try hiding the whole work area behind hinged doors, perhaps in an alcove, or make or adapt a cupboard to include space for a computer, with a sliding shelf for the keyboard if you want. The cupboard will need to be deep enough and there should be room for the heat generated by the hard-drive and monitor to escape.

85

entertaining thoughts

We all watch TV and appreciate a good sound system but we don't always like looking at them or having them clutter up the living room when they are not in use. There are ways of making them blend in though.

• Don't position seating around the TV: it gives it too much emphasis and looks odd when the TV isn't on. Instead, bring the TV to the seating area on a trolley or wheeled cabinet, but don't forget that cables and aerials will come with the TV.

• Some TVs and sound systems are now sleek accessories that enhance a stylish interior. You could even have a wide-screen TV professionally set into the wall.

• Store CD players, speakers and small TVs on open shelves. They will look less conspicuous with books and other objects alongside.

• TV cabinets incorporating storage for music systems, CDs, video tapes and DVDs are back in fashion. If you can't find one you like, have it made or adapt a cupboard, large box or chest. Don't forget to cut holes for the cables.

cable control

To avoid a tangle of unsightly cables and wires, keep wires for aerials and speakers either under the floor or in plastic conduit fixed to the skirting board (see 18). Feed computer cables through flexible plastic sleeves, or tie them up with plastic wire tags and tuck them out of sight.

storage matters

De-cluttering is all the rage, and while not everyone feels the need for a complete purge, most of us admit to having too much stuff and are happy to whittle down our possessions as part of a scheme to re-decorate or re-design a room. Start editing your possessions before you decide on storage needs: not only will you have a clearer idea of what your requirements are, you may also find there is less to store. Once you have finished decorating and are putting things back and adding finishing touches, you may well find yourself happily throwing out more things that suddenly don't look right, or spoil the effect. Most people are amazed, and often dismayed, at the amount of 'stuff' they accumulate, which is why storage has become a big issue and there is no shortage of products or suggestions that promise to transform you into a paragon of orderliness and your home into a picture of perfect tidiness.

de-clutter

De-cluttering is good for you. Getting rid of unwanted items will lighten the load on your mind as well as on your shelves.

don't fuss

Don't be tempted by gimmicky sets of small drawers or containers as these, in turn, can become a storage problem.

box clever

Boxes are great – but avoid small ones, and don't stack them too high as you will always want whatever is in the bottom one.

limited edition

Instead of increasing your storage space try reducing it. You will be surprised at how many things you can do without.

big is beautiful

Sorting things into bags, boxes or files and putting those together in one large container keeps things looking neat.

access

Be careful: your enthusiastic filing and organising may make things less accessible. Keep frequently used things within easy reach.

don't forget

Stashing everything away may look and feel great but it's easy to forget what's where, especially if you have gone for matching files and boxes. Labels will help.

safety instructions

Make sure that any hazardous liquids or flammable hobby materials are stored so they can't leak or give off dangerous fumes. Watch for heat damage caused by things placed too near the fireplace, pipework or radiators, and protect precious documents from insects and vermin by keeping them in airtight conditions.

walk-in-storage

Being able to store everything in a single walk-in space is a luxury, but not impossible if you have a small room or large cupboard opening off your living room.

please put it away

You can but ask!

head over heart

There are some things that we all accumulate, so how can you possibly deal with them?

magazines

These build up with alarming speed. Go through them cutting out articles you want to keep, but if you don't have time for that, get rid of them – except, of course, for any favourite or historic issues and any old or very rare ones.

photographs

Throwing away photographs is very difficult. Start by discarding poor quality ones, followed by any that make people look ugly, but never part with pictures of your, or your children's childhood. If you have photographs that recall unhappy memories, give them to someone for safe keeping instead of throwing them away.

paperwork

If you have a workspace in the living room, keep on top of paperwork and have a good, filing system so things look tidy. Put papers that you need to keep in a smart 'to file' container and tackle it every few months, then you'll find you can get rid of much of it with a clear conscience. Store what you can on space-saving discs.

treasures

We all have treasured objects with sentimental value. They add personality to a living room but too many spoil the effect. So edit your collection and select a few favourites for display. Store the rest in a 'treasure chest'.

books

If you can bear to part with any of your books, the best place to start is with those you know you won't read again, and any with outdated information or on subjects you are no longer interested in. Otherwise, keep on adding bookshelves!

88 out in the open

Open storage is a great way of combining storage with display and is suitable for anything from books and files to collections of ceramics and treasures.

freestanding storage

As these systems aren't fixed to the wall, they are versatile and can be moved around easily. They also make ideal room dividers. Most consist of wood or metal frames to which shelves or sometimes cupboards are fixed. They come in a variety of heights and materials including wood, glass, laminate and metal, and vary from plain and budget to expensive and smart. New designs may incorporate coloured laminated panels and veneers.

brackets and battens

The ubiquitous metal bracket system is one of the easiest ways of putting up shelves. They can be any length, and as long as you use enough uprights, there is no limit to how wide you can go. Styles vary, with some more sophisticated and expensive. Shelves on wooden battens are a neat way of filling an alcove. Use a batten on the back wall too for extra strength.

floating shelves

The 'floating' shelf is a box-like construction with no visible means of support that looks very 'now'. It is fixed to the wall with a concealed batten and bolt system. Buy them off-the-shelf (but they need a secure fixing, so are unsuitable for poor-quality walls and some partition walls) or have them made to your own specifications.

take a bookcase

• Although the quality and finish of cheap bookshelves may not be perfect, once they are full of books and other objects their failings are not so obvious. The best way to use them is boldly: a row of full-height bookcases along one wall, for example. Using small units in isolation looks bitty and will highlight their inadequacies. Stick to perfectly plain styles, and consider painting them the same colour as the walls.

• Look in antique markets and junk shops for old, solid-wood, bookcases and charming painted ones. Glass-fronted

bookcases look very special and will make choosing a book even more of a pleasure.

• Go to a smart furniture retailer for refined and elegant contemporary designs in the latest shapes, materials and colours and with the newest design details. Look out for double bookcases with two sets of shelving, the front set on runners for ease of access. Watch out also for the extraordinary 'Bookworm' designed by Ron Arad, which comprises a length of coloured plastic fixed to the wall in a dramatic curve.

making ordinary shelves look smart

• Use thick, chunky wood, reclaimed wood or even scaffolding planks in place of the more usual laminated or chipboard shelves.

• Shelves will be stronger and look deeper with a wooden lip attached to the front. This can be painted or you could use a special wood to make a feature of it. Metal strip is another option for an industrial look.

• Buy well finished, thick shelves in interesting materials to smarten up an ordinary bracket system.

modular storage

Modular storage systems offer a practical and versatile solution to your storage requirements. Not only do they allow you to put together a combination that will fit your specific needs and the layout of your room, but they are also available in a variety of configurations including open shelves and the option to add solid or glass doors to open box-like shapes. Most systems have backs and are available in square or rectangular formations, and many offer modules for the specialised storage of CDs and videos, as well as the TV and music system. Most are freestanding and comparatively easy to move around so you can alter the configuration to suit your changing whims and requirements; extra shelves, doors or whole units can be added as needed, or when funds allow. The range of styles and materials is now very wide from the most basic, simple cube system to more sophisticated designs, which look less modular and more like smart furniture, with styles ranging from contemporary to traditional. Modular storage is perfect for homes where fixing to walls is difficult or not allowed (in rented accommodation, for example), and as it is not built-in, you can take it with you when you move. Be imaginative in how you use them: pile them high, keep them low or stack them ziggurat-style.

built-in and bespoke

Although the choice of storage is huge it is not always possible to find exactly what you want. Built-in furniture and fittings maximise the use of space and can be designed to fit your specific storage and design requirements. DIY stores and builder's merchants have a wide range of products that enable you to construct anything from a simple shelf to a whole wall of cupboards. Many of the components are very good value for money and as long as you keep things simple there is no reason why they can't be used to create stylish storage in a living room. However, for large built-in cupboards and more complex designs, the workmanship must be perfect: a badly hung door will spoil and cheapen the whole effect. A professional carpenter will ensure a good finish and may be willing to design and build an altogether more sophisticated system. Better quality materials and skilled craftsmanship with details such as bevelled or rounded edges and proper joints can turn built-in shelving into beautiful fittings. There are lots of small designer/maker companies, so why not commission an individual piece of furniture such as a computer or TV cabinet, made to your own specifications?

three style hints

1 • ceiling-to-floor doors are modern and minimal
2 • good fittings, such as hinges and handles, turn ordinary into special
3 • good finishes on paintwork or wood turn the simplest job into quality workmanship

91
behind closed doors

Putting things away has many advantages. They are out of sight, don't gather dust and won't detract from the decor. Some items are always safer and better off behind closed doors.

wall of cupboards

The ultimate in modern storage thinking, a wall of cupboards can take care of all your storage requirements, from paperwork to spare bedding. Choose from wall-to-ceiling cupboards with virtually invisible doors painted to match the walls, or solid wood or wood veneer doors in a dark or grainy finish. If you prefer, the doors can be of varying sizes and colours, or you could opt for a combination of solid and glass doors, drawers, pigeonholes and open shelves. Although a wall of cupboards is normally fitted along one wall it can also be used as a room divider. Access can be from one or both sides and you could have a different finish on each. Either have a carpenter build your wall of cupboards (see 90), use modular storage (see 89), or cover the wall in plain, off-the peg kitchen units.

big cupboards

A single beautiful or unusual cupboard can be the focal point of a room as well as provide valuable storage space. The choice is vast, from simple modern styles to country-style presses and armoires complete with original worn paintwork. You don't have to have a big room to house a big cupboard: it can work well in a small room too, especially if you keep other furnishings to a minimum.

three cupboard styles

1 • Modern: plain and simple, tall and slim; look for richly coloured, grainy wood, or pale 'blond' wood; etched glass doors.

2 • Antique: French armoires, sometimes painted white, with decorative mouldings and occasionally glass doors; utilitarian linen-presses in stripped or painted pine.

3 • Shaker style: over-sized Shaker presses in traditional cherrywood are fiendishly expensive but magnificent. They will definitely impose their style on the room.

chests

You can stow a lot of stuff in a big box or chest, and also use it as a table or seat. Old ones are best: look for sea chests and blanket boxes in mellowed wood or with painted decoration. Old storage crates look great in a minimal interior.

Chests of drawers may be used mostly for clothing but they are very good for storing other things from CDs to art materials. Many modern designs are now made for use in living spaces, while a large old or antique chest of drawers can look good anywhere.

five fresh ideas for storage

1 • New or old changing-room lockers make great storage solutions. Choose from rows of small cupboards or tall, thin ones.

2 • Strong metal flight cases with reinforced metal edges and corners with chunky wheels are used by rock bands and photographers for storing and transporting equipment, but they can look very stylish in a living room.

3 • Old hospital and medical equipment is perfect for the utilitarian, industrial look and is very solid and well made. Look for metal, glass-fronted wall cabinets, and large metal cupboards. Some shops and dealers specialise in this type of salvage or you may be lucky and find examples in second-hand shops and markets.

4 • As well as big wooden or metal cupboards you may be lucky enough to find an old-fashioned filing system or vintage shop fittings. Old wooden filing cabinets are more difficult to find but the newer metal types can be cleaned and repainted.

5 • School cupboards often end up in junk shops. They will respond to a good clean and a coat of paint. Wood-veneered fittings from the sixties and seventies look very now.

92

storage special **books, magazines and CDs**

baskets

A strong, well-made basket always looks attractive and is a great place to store your newspapers and magazines. Large ones will hold a week's worth but smaller, narrower shapes are perfect for keeping current reading handy. Look for seagrass and colourful designs in plastic.

pigeonholes

Pigeonholes are great for storage and allow you to file anything, from letters, bills and work papers to CDs, videos or books, by name, category, title or colour. You can find them in a variety of sizes from small, wall-mounted CD and video storage to larger freestanding pieces of furniture with holes large enough for magazines and books.

on the floor

If you file everything away you may forget to read it. A tall stack of magazines on a bare floor looks very minimal, and if you are short of wall space or want to keep your living room fashionably bare, arrange your books on the floor around the walls.

double agent dual-purpose storage

locker space
Take a tip from boats and caravans and use stowage underneath a window seat or bench seating.

modular units
Instead of stacking modular storage units, place a single row around the walls and use the top for display and seating.

favourite things
Don't waste the space offered by collections of baskets, boxes, suitcases, hatboxes, large pots, tins, bags or other receptacles – fill them up!

storage ideas for work and paperwork

wooden filing cabinets
These are altogether smarter than the metal variety and suit traditional living rooms but their sturdy good looks also look chic in a minimal environment.

matching stationery
If your paperwork is kept on open shelves it will look organised and stylish in matching sets of files and boxes. These are available in a wide range of colours and patterns but stick to neutral and discreet unless you want to make a feature of them.

strong boxes
Look in antique markets and junk shops for old tin trunks and boxes as used by solicitors to store clients' papers. If you prefer new there are plenty of modern versions in plain and coloured metal. Not only do they look good, they will also help keep precious documents safe from damp and fire.

display your treasures

shop fittings

Old shop fittings and display cases are wonderful for storing as well as displaying collections. The best come from old-fashioned drapery or haberdashery shops, are beautifully made and have glass-fronted compartments and pull-out drawers. It is worth investigating shop-fitting suppliers who may be prepared to sell you one of the latest modern equivalents.

dressers

The dresser never really goes out of fashion and is the perfect way to show off a collection of china, but it looks equally good filled with any treasured objects. Ideal for living/dining rooms, the large traditional styles still look wonderful but there are simpler, modern designs for a more sophisticated look.

long shelf

A single narrow shelf all round the wall provides an excellent display space for a large collection of almost anything, but is particularly good for ceramics and china, and you can also hang cups and jugs from hooks screwed underneath.

picture perfect

gallery style

Take a tip from the galleries where pictures are often hung in a single line at eye level. Keep all the frames and sizes the same and it will look very modish.

picture shelf

Prop pictures against the wall on a narrow shelf with a lip or fascia to prevent them from sliding off. This saves the bother of nails, screws or hooks and you can change the display whenever you fancy.

big frames

Putting a group of photographs in a big frame is not a new idea but to make them look more grown-up, have them professionally framed and mounted, and be adventurous with your choice of frames.

bulldog clips

Keep up a running commentary on your life by clipping your latest snaps to bulldog clips and hanging them from nails on the wall. Devote a whole wall to the idea for real impact.

freestanding

Invest in proper photograph frames in various sizes and materials. While you may not have a grand piano to display them on you could use a console table, a shelf or the mantelpiece. It is nice to be able to pick them up and examine them closely once in a while.

3

part three

keeping it fresh

97 time to come clean

If you spend time, money and effort creating a stylish living room it makes sense to look after it. Cleaning has become fashionable, with humble housework now imbued with a spiritual dimension. The pared-down look has been partly influenced by a widening interest in Zen philosophy, which not only encourages us to clear our lives of unnecessary clutter but also exhorts us to take pleasure in daily tasks such as the rituals of everyday cleaning. While this may not convince you to pick up your duster, you can probably relate to a wish for a little more peace, harmony and order in your life, and for many the home is the place to find it.

Increasing interest in interiors has resulted in much higher standards of tidiness and cleanliness. Unfortunately, minimalism shows the dirt and keeping up appearances can take a lot of time and effort. Maintaining perfection as seen in the pages of magazines is unrealistic and can prevent you from enjoying your home; however, cleaning and restoring can be therapeutic, which means that it benefits you as well as your living room.

three good reasons for cleaning

1 • it's good for your health
House dust is known to aggravate respiratory problems and allergies, stale air can contain germs as well as fumes and smoke, and hard and soft surfaces can harbour bacteria.

2 • it's good for your soul
Busy lives can make us oblivious to our surroundings and we forget to appreciate them. Spending time cleaning will reacquaint you with your living space and possessions and can restore the spirits . A well-maintained home will bestow a sense of calm, order and well-being.

3 • it's good for your home
Furnishings, floors and floor coverings will last longer, and look better, if they are cared for. Dirt and dust damage surfaces and textiles, while materials such as wood dry out in a centrally heated atmosphere. Living room floors are subjected to hard wear and need regular attention to keep them in good condition.

three clean approaches

1 • the Zen way
Zen and the art of household maintenance involves taking pleasure in the daily tasks of cleaning and arranging your possessions carefully and thoughtfully.

2 • the quick way
Open a window, put on some lively music, plump up the cushions and get hold of a feather duster and dustbuster to give everything a quick, freshening once-over.

3 • the easy way
Pay someone to do your cleaning but make sure they do things your way. Keep a check on the cleaning products they use, especially if your living room houses valuable furniture or expensive materials.

three dusting tips

1 • Slightly dampen the duster: dust is for picking up not for spreading around

2 • Wash or shake out dusters after use otherwise you will put the old dust back

3 • Use an artist's paintbrush to dust between the keys on your keyboard

three useful hints

1 • Put cushions in the sun to fluff them up

2 • Clean windows with just warm water and a squirt of washing-up liquid: ammonia-based cleaners leave smears

3 • Clean glass vases by filling them with warm water and dropping in one or two denture-cleaning tablets

spring cleaning

Spring awakens all sorts of things in us and while your fancy may turn to thoughts other than cleaning, the sun streaming through a smeary living-room window onto piles of dust might just spur you into action. Spring cleaning offers an opportunity to pay attention to items that get short shrift during the rest of the year, such as carpets, curtains, cushions and upholstery. Solid floors will also benefit from some extra maintenance, as will dust-attracting fixtures and fittings like light fittings, TVs, entertainment sytems, computers and other electrical equipment. This is also a good time to show respect for antiques if you are lucky enough to have them as well as for any other valuable items that may require special treatment or just some tender loving care.

celebrate

Ancient spring festivals of cleansing and purification held to welcome the season of new growth included several rituals in the home. So instead of facing this annual event with trepidation, why not hold your own festival and turn it into a celebration rather than a chore? Set a date and get in supplies of cloths, cleansers, mops and buckets and rubber gloves, and check that the vacuum cleaner and the washing machine are up to the job. Lay in stocks of delicious food to keep you going and a special treat for when all is done and dusted. Alternatively, cleaning companies are springing up everywhere, so you may opt for paying them to do your cleaning for you – but you can still celebrate your clean, fresh living space when they've finished and gone home.

five useful aids

1 • long handles

Long-handled brushes, feather dusters and mops are good for clearing dust, fluff and cobwebs from ceilings and picture rails or underneath large items of heavy or fixed furniture.

2 • vacuum cleaner

A good vacuum cleaner with a comprehensive set of tools is vital for thorough spring-cleaning. The tools are perfect for sucking dust from edges, corners, skirting boards and around window frames, and are ideal for cleaning and refreshing curtains and upholstery. Essential for carpets and natural floor coverings, they are also efficient on bare floors – but be careful they don't scratch. If you have a very expensive tufted carpet take care which type of vacuum cleaner you choose as some of the super-powered ones may pull the tufts out.

3 • step ladder

Pre-empt any excuses for not getting into those corners by having a step ladder handy. Survey the room from the top step and you will be able to see the bits you have missed.

4 • dust sheets

Cover precious furnishings and other items to protect them from dust, splashes or accidental damage. You may also want to cover carpets and posh floors to keep them safe.

5 • toothbrush

Sometimes a toothbrush is simply the best way to winkle out that stubborn bit of dirt or dust.

general advice

Special living-room surfaces deserve special care, so put on those rubber gloves and get started.

floors

Now is the time to re-wax, re-oil, or re-seal bare floors, but remove the dirt first or you may damage the surface or get a build-up of products. If you have a newly installed floor, follow the supplier's advice. Many flooring materials are pre-treated and using the wrong product could result in damage. Carpets and natural floor coverings need a thorough vacuuming, including all edges and corners. Move furniture to get underneath. Stains and dirt may require special attention – often best done by a professional cleaning company.

furniture

Cleaning varies according to material, age and value. Follow supplier's instructions and if unsure about an antique, ask an expert. Wood sealed with varnish only requires wiping with a damp cloth, while unsealed wood needs a barely damp cloth followed by waxing or oiling. Wash plastic laminates and moulded plastics with a mild detergent and gently remove stubborn dirt or stains with a non-abrasive cleaner.

curtains and upholstery

Lightweight curtains and covers can be laundered and heavier fabrics cleaned professionally, but not every year as this can shorten their life. Just vacuum using a brush tool. Good-quality upholstery should be professionally steam-cleaned.

paintwork

Don't get carried away washing paintwork: you are only removing surface dirt not preparing it for painting. Just wash with a mild detergent solution.

99

five ideas for the five senses

1 • see

Follow the Zen practice of placing one special object – a single flower, a smooth pebble or something made by your child – in its own setting in your living room so you can meditate on its beauty.

2 • smell

Enjoy the fresh, natural smell of scented plants, flowers and herbs, of clean fabrics, beeswax polish, a bowl of apples and fresh air.

3 • feel

Feel the effect on your skin of soft, cashmere, cool, crisp cotton, coarse, linen and soft velvets and silks and enjoy the feel of a smooth stone floor on bare feet, the breeze from an open window or the warming comfort of a flickering fire.

4 • hear

Enjoy the sound of silence by insisting on bare feet or slippers and using sound-absorbent curtains, rugs or wallhangings.

5 • taste

Your taste buds will be more receptive in an environment of natural materials free from harmful chemicals and distracting artificial smells or smoke.

100

seasonal changes

Everyone loves a warm and cosy living room in winter and one filled with fresh air and sunlight in summer. Underline the changing seasons with these ideas.

natural cycles

Busy modern living makes us less sensitive to seasonal changes, which harms our sense of well-being. Connect to the changing seasons by decorating with seasonal flowers and plants or other natural objects – a fir cone, a few autumn leaves, a collection of seashells or some seasonal fruit.

light

Be aware of the changing quality of light and the position of the sun throughout the year. Welcome in the summer by taking down heavy window coverings and make the most of the lighter evenings by sitting and unwinding gently in the restful twilight rather than turning on the lights.

101

meet an artist – buy a work of art!

index

acknowledgements

Picture credits

1 Ray Main/Mainstream/C2 Architects; 2 left Ray Main/ Mainstream; 2 centre Ray Main/Mainstream/ Architect Brian Ma Siy; 2 right Ray Main/Mainstream/ Designer Dominic Richards; 3 left Ray Main/Mainstream/ Designer Phillipe Starck; 3 centre Ray Main/Mainstream/ Chateau De Massillan; 3 right Ray Main/Mainstream; 4 above Ray Main/Mainstream/ The Inside Design Studios; 4 above centre Ray Main/ Mainstream; 4 below centre Ray Main/Mainstream; 4 below Ray Main/Mainstream/ Smart Intergration; 7 Ray Main/Mainstream/Ligne Roset; 8 Ray Main/ Mainstream; 9 Ray Main/ Mainstream; 10-11 Ray Main/ Mainstream/Maisonette; 12-13 Ray Main/Mainstream/ Mulberry; 13 Ray Main/ Mainstream; 14 Ray Main/ Mainstream/Guinivere; 15 Ray Main/Mainstream; 16 Ray Main/Mainstream/Architect Paul Forbes; 17 Ray Main/ Mainstream; 18-19 Ray Main/ Mainstream/Pearl Lowe; 20-21 below Ray Main/Mainstream/ ArchitectLittmanGoddard Hogarth; 20-21 above Paul Massey/ Mainstream;22-23 Ray Main/ Mainstream; 24-25 RayMain/Mainstream/Archi- tects Zegna&Biochetto; 26 Ray Main/Mainstream; 27 Ray Main/Mainstream; 28-29 Ray Main/Mainstream/Mulberry; 31 Ray Main/Mainstream/ Mathmos; 32-33 Ray Main/ Mainstream; 34-35 Ray Main/ Mainstream; 37 Ray Main/ Mainstream; 38-39 Ray Main/ Mainstream; 41 below Ray Main/Mainstream/20th Century design; 41 above Ray Main/Mainstream; 42-43 Ray Main/Mainstream/Designer www.shaunclarkson.com; 42 Ray Main/Mainstream/ Designer ww.shaunclarkson. com; 44-45 Ray Main/ Mainstream; 45 Ray Main/ Mainstream; 46-47 Ray Main/ Mainstream/Designer William Yeoward; 48 Ray Main/ Mainstream/Architect Phillip Meadowcroft;49 Ray Main/ Mainstream; 50 Ray Main/ Mainstream;51 Ray Main/Mainstream/Architect Oliver Morgan; 52-53 Ray Main/ Mainstream/Millersuk.com;53 above Ray Main/ Mainstream; 53 below Ray Main/ Mainstream/Millersuk.com; 57 Ray Main/Mainstream/ M.K Architects; 58 Ray Main/ Mainstream/Dev UsickHeal Associates; 60 Ray Main/ Mainstream/Designer Dominic Richards; 61 Ray Main/ Mainstream/Architects Gregory Phillips; 62-63 Ray Main/Mainstream/Peter Wadley Architects; 63 Ray Main/Mainstream; 64 Ray Main/Mainstream/Barratta Design; 65 Ray Main/Mainstream; 66 Ray Main/Mainstream/Abraham & Thakore; 67 Paul Massey/Mainstream; 69 Ray Main/Mainstream/Chateau De Massillan; 70-71 above Ray Main/Mainstream; 70-71 below Paul Massey/ Mainstream; 71 Ray Main/ Mainstream;72 main Ray Main/Mainstream; 72 inset Paul massey/Mainstream;74- 75 Ray Main/Mainstream/ Designer Jo Warman; 76 Ray Main/Mainstream/Architects McDowel&Benedetti; 77 Ray Main/Mainstream/Architects McDowel&Benedetti; 78 Ray Main/Mainstream; 79 Ray Main/Mainstream; 81 Ray Main/Mainstream/Designer Phillipe Starck; 82-83 Ray Main/Mainstream/Designer Isokon; 85 left Ray Main/ Mainstream;85 below right Ray Main/Mainstream; 85 above right Ray Main/ Mainstream/Designer Catherine Memmi; 86-87 Ray Main/ Mainstream; 87 Ray Main/ Mainstream; 88 Ray Main/ Mainstream/Designer Craig Allen/Linley; 89 below left Ray Main/Mainstream/Designer Michael Sodeaux; 89 above right Ray Main/Mainstream/ Architect Brian Ma Siy; 90 Ray Main/Mainstream/Designer James Knapp; 91 Paul Massey/ Mainstream; 92 Ray Main/ Mainstream; 93 above left Ray Main/Mainstream; 93 below left Ray Main/Mainstream; 93 above right Ray Main/ Mainstream; 93 below right Paul Massey/Mainstream; 94 below left Ray Main/ Mainstream; 94 above right Ray Main/Mainstream/ Architect Simon Conder; 95 Ray Main/Mainstream; 96 below Ray Main/Mainstream; 96 above Ray Main/ Mainstream/John F Rolf Design and Build; 97 Ray Main/ Mainstream 99 Ray Main/ Mainstream/Sergison Bates Architects; 100 Ray Main/ Mainstream; 101 right Ray Main/Mainstream; 101 left Ray Main/Mainstream; 103 right Ray Main/Mainstream; 102-103 Ray Main/Mainstream/ Design dalziel-pow; 104 Ray Main/Mainstream; 105 Ray Main/Mainstream 106-107 Ray Main/Mainstream/Smart Integration 108 Ray Main/ Mainstream/20th Century design; 109 above Ray Main/ Mainstream; 109 below Ray Main/Mainstream; 111 Ray Main/Mainstream; 113 Ray Main/Mainstream/20th Century design; 114-115 Ray Main/Mainstream; 116 Ray Main/Mainstream; 117 Ray Main/Mainstream/Maisonette